Contents

Preface

Burundi, 1999: The deserted beach was as beautiful as anywhere. Ed and I splashed into the fresh water under the baking sun and blue sky, with the rugged mountains looming over us on either side of the lake. We were throwing a tennis ball to each other, diving around to catch it as it skimmed across the surface. We were enjoying some time off, bursting with energy and full of life. Then 30 yards away a hippo slowly raised his head above the water and quietly observed us. Hippos kill more humans than any other animal in Africa, but we didn't really register the potential danger. We just turned gingerly in his direction, hushed our voices, and watched him, cherishing the moment. What a beautiful world we lived in...

It sounds exotic and idyllic – and I guess it was – except that in the distance up in the hills above the city we could see the outline of a 'displacement' camp of tens of thousands of people. They had been forcefully rounded up and lived in conditions of unimaginable squalor. There were fifty-six such camps around the capital. The one I managed to enter had 40,000 people in it, and ten people were dying there each day, day after day, week after week. Incidents of rape were commonplace, and AIDS was spreading like wildfire. The rebels had just sent down the chopped-off heads of the soldiers they had killed, provoking the latter to retaliate by killing forty civilians on the way to market. What a sick and twisted world we lived in...

The world is indeed a beautiful place, and at the same time a sick and twisted one. We would later look up at the sun setting over those mountains and think: 'God, what an awesome creation, and yet what a horrific mess we have made of it!'

Such has been Ed Walker's world over the last number of years, as he has travelled and worked in the most seemingly God-forsaken and undesirable spots on the planet. I shared some of his early adventures before he moved on to fresh challenges. Wherever he has been, living in war zones or areas of extreme hunger, the scenes before him have elicited many extremes of emotion and gut-wrenchingly raw questions. In the following pages you will be deeply shocked, moved, challenged and cheered by multiple stories of both the best and the worst of humanity on the African continent.

Ed's zest for life, irrepressible sense of humour, compassion for the marginalized, and heart-searching quest for some sort of coherent answers to the questions life throws up at him all make for a stirring and uncomfortable read which will hopefully lead each one of us to assess what our own contribution or role has been and might be in making a difference in this beautiful but sick and twisted world.

Simon Guillebaud

Foreword

We see it on the television news and it moves us – the half-starved child's tears in the refugee camp, the wide-eyed horror on the face of the genocide survivor – but to be there is another matter. In my travels with Tearfund, and through my own earlier experience on emergency relief programmes in Afghanistan and Somalia, I've seen enough to know that you cannot do this kind of work without being changed for ever.

Ed Walker has worked for Tearfund's Disaster Response teams in some of the most heart-breaking situations Africa has seen in recent years – Darfur, Sierra Leone, southern Sudan, Burundi, Rwanda, Northern Kenya and Liberia. Places where violence, brutality, hunger and fear were the norm.

This book takes us on a journey through the everyday challenges of relief work – the ups, the downs, the joys, the frustrations. It shows how determined action can save lives. But it also looks at the deeper issues, as Ed talks frankly about the challenge to his faith.

We've all asked the question: why does God allow suffering? But when you are confronted by extreme suffering day by day, it never goes away. Ed recounts his own painful questions as he cries out to God for understanding.

I believe this book offers us all a frank and thought-provoking perspective on service and suffering. Ed is vulnerable about his own anguish, his questions, his tears – and yes, his doubts. Believing in God doesn't mean we have all the answers. But Ed's story shows that sometimes when we face our doubts openly and honestly we find our faith emerges stronger. We can find hope, courage, and strength to persevere.

I hope that as you read this book your own understanding will be deepened, and you'll catch something of what drives Christians to compassionate action in forgotten places – the unfailing love of God.

Matthew Frost
Chief Executive, Tearfund

Acknowledgements

I am grateful to many people for reading and critiquing various drafts of this book: Gail Halley, Rachel Walker, Simon Guillebaud, Anthony and Jenny Savage, Graeme and Sue Walker, James Paul, Nick Swanepoel, Angus Murray, Mike Hollow and Darren Cormack. Thank you.

Mostly I am grateful to the editor, Tony Collins, for turning my dream into a reality and for seeing the potential of 'a book' amidst a sea of apostrophe and syntax errors. In the original draft I tried to keep myself out of the text as much as possible because the book is not about me but about the people I have met and the places I have been. Tony urged me otherwise. A part of me would prefer not to have so much of my life in there nor even a picture of me on the cover. I hope the reader understands that any reference to myself is in an attempt to draw people's attention to other issues which I believe are of value.

Introduction: Why Write?

Energized and excited, I land in Heathrow, place my visa card into my wallet and change the SIM card in my mobile phone to prepare for life in the UK.

In a similar way, I plug a new 'UK disk' into my brain, one that forgets where I have just come from and focuses on my British life. After early trips I might have been hurt if people didn't show interest. Later I learnt not to expect questions; now I prefer it if they are not asked. It is difficult to know how to ask questions about any life you can not easily relate to. Equally it is not always easy to explain; on some levels therefore it is easier not to discuss. Many of my friends work in the city and I am interested in the work they do and what their day looks like; but often I struggle to phrase the questions correctly and follow their answers. Sometimes, therefore, it is easier not to discuss.

Knowing how to 'pitch it' in church meetings is also difficult. Recently, I struggled to explain to a congregation, in five minutes, something of our security experiences over the past year. It involved tales of bullets, mortar fire, staff beatings and evacuations. Not something the average Surrey churchgoer can relate to, much as they earnestly try. On sitting back in the church seat, one is tempted to think of oneself as a freak: different, odd and difficult to relate to. So inevitably one ends up concealing that part which people struggle with, and learn to hide behind one's 'UK disk' still further.

However, the battle remains of trying to reconcile the

two worlds which I am privileged enough to straddle. I was walking through Liverpool Street, in the heart of London's financial district, in wonder at the tall buildings wiring millions of pounds across the world. Two hours later I was speaking to school children about 800,000 people killed in Rwanda and two million displaced Darfurians living in 'homes' barely larger than two school desks. We occupy a planet where both worlds exist simultaneously and yet neither my head nor heart can bracket them into a neat equation. They manifestly do not 'add up'. And so deep behind my UK disk there screams something which relates to the verse 'Shout it aloud, do not hold back. Raise your voice like a trumpet.'[1] People need to know what the world is like.

Some people use the medium of photos to talk about their experiences. I am drawn to writing. Through it one can explore and discover what is within. If we are a product of all we have been through, from the earliest childhood experience to last night's movie, then writing is catharsis, my way of getting what is inside, out. My way of grappling with that difficult equation.

Over the past few years I have read a number of books from journalists covering wars and disasters in Africa (such as George Alagiah's *A Passage to Africa* and Fergal Keane's *Letters Home*). Perhaps the authors were also trying to address the issue or equation. Their breadth of experience is greater than mine, though mine has been a similar (if more humble) journey. They write far better than I, but their analysis misses the vital spiritual perspective: Where is a God of love amidst suffering, war, murder, death? How and why did God create man capable of such inhumanity? They therefore leave an important leaf in our Christian understanding unturned by neglecting the spiritual dimension.

I have also read many helpful books which cover journeys of faith, doubt and searching. The authors may have been through worse than I have, or could imagine; however I have read few written in the context of war zones, relief work or drought-affected areas. Some answers to the above questions are attempted throughout the book and some are covered more specifically in chapters 8 and 9. Each chapter covers a different work contract, beginning with an overview of the region in which I am assigned.

The heat, dryness and tension of the places worked have sometimes made it feel like a 'scorched earth'. This phrase is in Isaiah (58:11) and has also been used to describe some of the atrocities in southern Sudan ('scorched earth policy'). Often, when in the field, after the tension has been at its hottest, I have looked back to try to find God amidst that 'scorched earth' and some of those reflections are covered in this book.

The thought of writing a book makes me cringe in a profound way. I find it embarrassing and scary for I discuss subjects about which I feel unqualified to write...not least theology. I am, however, encouraged by two verses: 'It is the glory of God to conceal a matter; to search out a matter is the glory of kings.'[2] 'He rewards those who earnestly seek him.'[3] God seems to affirm the dignity of searching, not just the finding. I am a searcher. There may be answers, very obvious to the reader, which remain 'concealed' from me. Maybe also readers disagree with some of the conclusion I draw. I hope these people will be gracious enough to validate the process of searching, if not the results themselves.

An English bishop wrote on the subject of doubt.[4] His argument went something like this: 'God gave us our minds and also guaranteed us his love. These two assurances liberate us to explore dark avenues of doubt while certain we can return to the open door of God's love.' Ironically it is through embracing and exploring these doubts that our faith can grow. My doubts are regular companions and are explored in this book.

As a remedy to doubts we are at times exhorted to 'lean not on [our] own understanding'[5] and reminded that our thoughts and ways are not his thoughts and ways.[6] Yet God also gave us a mind. The challenge then, is to blend receiving the kingdom of God like a little child[7] with using our adult intellect to enhance our faith. This book is partly a record of a personal journey of intellectual doubts and (not very childlike) trust in a God of love, sometimes in the face of extreme evidence to the contrary. It was written over eight and a half years of living and working in war- and drought-related 'disasters'.

I would understand if people (especially those sceptical of faith) reacted oddly against parts of this book; for at times it argues against things I believe in. All I can say is that it is an honest account of my thoughts and faith and how they have deepened and strengthened. My faith is that mysterious, unfathomable entity dwelling deep in the midst and core of me, too inexplicable to be captured and tied-down by words, yet extremely real, tangible and trustworthy. While doubts are regularly with me, my faith is my most treasured companion. I would urge everyone to explore their doubts in an effort to find their faith.

Finally, I am the first to admit how lucky I am in doing the work I do. It has brought me a life of great richness. It is also a 'sexy' form of employment: When I sit at a dinner party or wedding and explain what I 'do' I often receive a positive reaction. At times one is put on a false pedestal, which is both flattering and deceiving. Recently an event enabled me to catch a humbling glimpse of myself afresh; I saw something of who I really am, and the sins which God sees in me: a revolting mixed cauldron of pride, lust, arrogance, vanity and much more. I related more clearly than ever before to Paul's self-portrait: surely I am 'the worst of sinners'[8]. It was in that state of disgust and brokenness that I felt closer to God's grace and love than I had for a long time. Maybe also man's sinfulness and the hope God offers might come together somewhere in this book.

Notes

1. Isaiah 58:1.
2. Proverbs 25:2.
3. Hebrews 11:6.
4. I believe it was an old Bishop of Bath and Wells in an edition of *Daily Light* but I have not been able to trace it or his name.
5. Proverbs 3:5.
6. Isaiah 55:8.
7. Mark 10:15.
8. 1 Timothy 1:16.

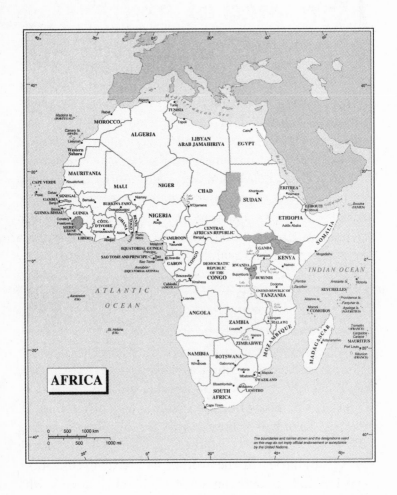

AFRICA

I Dreamed of Africa

Lying on my bed in the final term of university I read Kuki Gallmann's book *I Dreamed of Africa*. Often very moved by her words, I too dreamed of Africa: the adventure, the wildlife, meeting and understanding the different cultures, the music, the people.

I had twice before visited Africa – one trip to Kenya with my parents aged ten and one as a student to teach in a village in Nigeria. I assumed that, with a degree, the next step was to get a job and therefore my chance to spend a long time there had mainly gone. I might manage a few visits over the years but essentially I assumed I had missed the boat and was destined for UK-based employment. However I still found myself praying 'Lord, if it be your will, I would love to be over there – to work, to learn and to understand'.

But also there lay within me a passionate desire to give back something of my good fortune. Many a time I pondered on the fluke of being born into my background. Of the billions of babies born – what are the odds of landing the gifts I received: a middle-class family in one of the richest countries in the world, an excellent education, capable and functioning body and mind, parents who loved me and each other, my mother tongue being the dominant language in the world and so on. At twenty-two it felt as if the world was my oyster: well-paid jobs were available, my passport could get me to almost any country in the world and I could afford the ticket. Compared to the millions born each year into squalor and poverty (some of which I had witnessed in Nigeria and the Philippines) I felt undeservedly lucky, almost to the point of a guilt complex. Is it fair that I should be born with so much? Why did I deserve it? What made me so special that at twenty-two the world was such a free space whilst millions of my contemporaries were imprisoned by poverty and a lack of education.

For the first twenty-two years of my life I had done nothing but take. From day one I required the full attention of my mother, I had required the best part of twenty years to be looked after, to feed, to clothe, to discipline – when my mother was not giving to me it usually meant someone else was, mainly my school, paid for by my father. The school was filled with teachers working hard to get the best out of me. A year off was essentially a selfish pursuit. I wanted mainly to please myself, to indulge in travel, excitement and just 'being away'. Then came university – more teachers, paid for this time by taxpayers...and on and on. I felt the burden of the enormous investment required to get me to graduate status and often I would react by pompously saying to myself that if I had spent the first twenty-two years receiving, it was only fair, about time and almost my duty, to spend some of the next decades 'giving back' ... whatever that meant.

On leaving school I had spent a year overseas in Australia, a year I thoroughly loved but also one during which I missed home enormously. If it had taught me anything it was that home is where the heart is and that for me was definitely England, family, friends, and somewhere with a history that spanned more than a handful of decades. I loved travelling – I loved the thought of going overseas and visiting many parts of the world – but not long term. I did not want to bear the pain of another year overseas.

While working for a charitable organization in London, I prayed hard about where God wanted me and time passed slowly. Development work rather than relief or disaster work always interested me. However, through the encouragement of a friend, my speculative application followed by four interviews got me onto Tearfund's Disaster Response register. Being part of the register didn't involve very much at all. I would continue with my job while avidly scanning the paper trying to find a disaster. I found myself in a strange state of mind where, like a medical student looking forward to their time on A&E and hoping for accidents, I was hoping for some major world disaster and then struggling with my conscience as a result. One night I sat watching a documentary on Sierra Leone, I can still recollect vivid images of a rebel soldier, in the heart of the capital Freetown, shooting an hysterical woman in the leg. 'So is this the type of place Tearfund will send you then?' 'Erm...not sure.'

Tearfund had been a charity I had long been interested in and supported. I remember the stalls at my church when I was growing up. At 18 I sponsored a child through Tearfund and then at university I went on a 'Transform' team to Belfast. I always felt my heart was more in line with their mission statement than almost any other charity. To serve Jesus Christ by serving the poor aroused something in me. It felt like the child who had grown up supporting Manchester United and then finally got to play for them. I still feel that to wear the Tearfund shirt, to represent God in my work, is an honour which inspires me to raise my game.

Suddenly things began to move very fast. Before I knew it I was swotting up on my French, doing logistics work in Tearfund HQ for a few weeks before flying off to Burundi for a first taste of relief work. The last few days were such a mad rush of activity that I could barely keep myself together. I was being orientated in the programme, trying to learn as many French words as my tiny brain could cram in, say all my goodbyes with mates in London, pack from my house in Cambridge and do all those irritating things like getting an international driver's licence. Somehow the flurry kept moving forward and, armed with a replacement fax machine, I was soon saying good-bye to my ever-faithful parents at Heathrow. They were, as ever, encouraging; loving me enough to keep their worries and concerns to themselves while allowing me to fly (both metaphorically and physically) with their full blessing and support.

My main recollection of the overnight flight is trying my hardest to read through the security document and learn the phonetic alphabet (Alpha, Bravo, Charlie, Delta, etc.). The stopover in Nairobi preceded the short flight into Bujumbura, the capital of Burundi. Nervous excitement, anxiety, and a desire to remain calm were foremost in my mind.

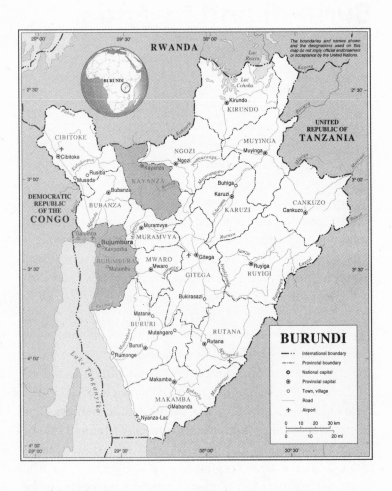

Population	8,090,068 (estimate 2006)	Religion	67% Christian, 10% Muslim, 23% indigenous
Population Growth	3.7%	Language	Kirundi and French
Prevalence of HIV	6% (estimate 2003)	Literacy	51%
People Living with HIV/AIDS	250,000	Life Expectancy	50

CHAPTER TWO

Burundi and Rwanda

Ever since I heard I was to sign a six-month contract for Burundi, I was fascinated by the country. I still am. It holds a special place in my heart beyond any other I have been to and I have returned twice to the country for a holiday. My six months turned into just under twelve and it was a year full of excitement, learning, and friendships.

Burundi is a tiny, densely populated country in the heart of Africa. Her post-independence history has been dominated by ethnic tension and fighting between the Tutsi and Hutu. There is also a third tribe called the Btwa (pronounced Batwa) that accounts for roughly 1 per cent of the population. The history is not dissimilar to that of Rwanda, though it is also unique. In both countries Tutsis have represented the minority; typically they have been characterized by different physiological features though there is no way to guarantee from sight which 'tribe' one belongs to. The stereotypical Tutsis are seen as taller and thinner. Historically they are nilotic[1] cattle herders. The Hutus are smaller and are historically thought to be Bantu arable farmers. Both tribes share the same villages and exactly the same language.

While Rwanda has tended, until post-genocide, to be ruled by Hutus, Burundi has predominantly been ruled by Tutsis. The Rwandan genocide was an attempt by the Hutus to exterminate the Tutsis. Burundi's history is more one of the Tutsi elite trying to hold on to power and purging the country of educated Hutu. The genocide in Rwanda lasted a matter of months, and since the refugees returned the country has been broadly stable. (It has been continuing to fight the war in Eastern Congo, but the interior has remained relatively calm). Burundi, by contrast, began her war following the elections of 1993 (before the Rwanda genocide), and continued until a peace accord in 2006. Sometimes it was referred to as a trickle genocide, sometimes just civil war. When I went there in May 1999 the statistics said that over 200,000 people had been killed. In the weekly UN security meetings which I attended scores of further deaths were always reported. In the next five years the war continued unabated, even intensified, and by 2004 papers began quoting 300,000 deaths. No one really knows how many have died; but it's a lot. 'The problem is...there is nobody counting, nobody taking names. You just bury the dead and move on.'[2]

When I arrived in May 1999, international sanctions had recently been lifted on Pierre Buyoya's Government after he seized power by a coup in 1996. A peace process was underway and people were broadly hopeful. Over the next year much of that hope began to evaporate as the fighting intensified and attacks on the roads and capital increased in ferocity and regularity.

Bujumbura, the capital city, was small, with districts utterly obliterated and abandoned in the course of the war. Despite that it continued to function as a small city, with a couple of large markets, a few posh residential areas, one Asian district and many slum areas.

In stark contrast to the nation's savage history, the country is stunningly beautiful. The capital sits on the north-eastern end of Lake Tanganika. Across the 30 kilometres of water, on the western side of the lake, towers Congo. She stands as a line of lush green mountains, looming over Bujumbura: high, stunning but also imposing and threatening. Behind the city, mirroring the image of Congo, stand the mountains that are Burundi, stretching down the eastern side of the lake – high, steep, lush, green, beautiful and perfect for guerrilla and rebel activity.

Through the eyes of a complete fresher, who had not been to a war zone (except Belfast), there seemed masses of armed soldiers and police. Signs of war were everywhere – entire districts were wiped out with every house either abandoned or ruined.

Worse than the physical effect, much of the impact of the war was insidious, it ran deeper than surface destruction. As I drove past a soldier, I would wonder at the trauma he was suffering and the psychological baggage the front-line had left in his tortured memory. There are many costs to a war – but how can one count the cost of the psychological trauma – the uncountable nightmares, the reduced ability to work and all the other symptoms which naturally result. In the West you would be able to obtain a certificate from a doctor, claim a post-traumatic stress disorder and receive compensation. In Burundi there are no such safeguards; the battle-weary have to battle on in order to survive.

A lot of the fighting in Burundi, as in Rwanda, had been low-budget. A high percentage of it was death by machete. Neighbour on neighbour, even family member on family member – and the incipient fight still rumbled on in 1999. There were regular reports of villages attacked with scores of people killed. Every Burundian was able to tell some horrific tale of slaughter or fleeing from rebels or terrifying attack; all seemed affected and almost all, I am sure, had witnessed death or war in the flesh.

Friends and colleagues at Tearfund, who I guess were representative of the population, told me many 'histoires', which give a flavour of the history:

Boniface told how his father, a Hutu, had been the finance minister for the country in the early 1970s. During a purge of educated and successful Hutus, his father feared for his life and so planned to flee with his family to America. About a week before they were due to fly, the family, staying out in their rural village home, heard a knock on the door. The soldiers asked for Boniface's father who followed them out and was never seen again. Burundi lost a talented minister and Boniface grew up penniless and fatherless. When the war broke out again in 1993 he fled to Kayanza (a town 90 kilometres to the north). Clearly intelligent, he was employed by Tearfund as a driver. Had his father lived, he would more than likely have grown up in America with a strong education – or in Burundi as a minister's son.

As Hutus, the majority of Celestian's extended family had been killed in his rural village. He was now responsible for supporting what remained of his family on his meagre salary. Pasteur saw a friend, ringed amidst flaming tyres, burnt to death. Willy walked through the city centre and saw a man clubbed to death in broad daylight.

A Burundian proverb refers to the 'smiling assassin' – the Burundian who smiles at you on the one hand and stabs you in the back with the other. Burundians themselves say they are very good at hiding their thoughts. In our team two staff reportedly did not get on. One was a

Hutu, the other a Tutsi. The Tutsi, so we were told, threatened to kill the Hutu. A few weeks later the two of them were chatting away amicably in the back of a vehicle. I shared this, delighted in the apparent reconciliation, with someone who knew far more than I. She told me not to be fooled; the animosity might still lurk beneath the surface.

But the above stories only tell of one aspect; they do not tell the whole picture. The Burundians are also very warm, kind people. My greatest joy came from the friendships I developed, the closeness I felt with them and their generosity towards me. Boniface and Pelagie would regularly invite me over for cards and a drink. Willy was another special friend, at times we would laugh so hard my ribs were splitting; I had the privilege of being with him when he was ill and sharing some moments of tears. It is hard to explain the love, warmth and security I felt from these friends just through doing the most normal of things: in sharing a meal, in teasing one another, in competing over a hand of cards – it was not so much the words we were saying; it was what we were not saying that mattered.

There are other stories, stories one hears less often but which also reveal the Burundian character. When the war broke out in 1993, Deo lived in the same village in which he was born and educated. He knew almost his entire village and almost his entire village knew him. Shortly after the fighting started, his two brothers were hacked to death with machetes. The people holding those machetes were people of Deo's own age, living in the same village, alike in every way...except that they were from a different 'tribe'. Deo struggled with every normal human reaction to those circumstances: bereavement, grief, loss; but also, understandably, a massive sense of bitterness, anger and a desire for revenge. At one stage he was seriously and determinedly plotting a fatal retribution.

Instead, he tells of going to the very people who had killed his brothers, with a Bible under his arm, and telling them that whilst once he was plotting revenge, he had managed to forgive them. Somewhere between the plotting and the forgiving he became a Christian. I do not know how long he struggled with these issues nor how long it took him to truly forgive. Sometimes looking at his tortured face I sensed it was not something he managed to do overnight. Whatever the process he went through he found that forgiving freed him from the prison of hatred, bitterness and revenge. I cannot begin to imagine how hard that must have been for him. I am not glossing over the issues of bringing people to justice, I am just telling the bare bones of an amazing story. Deo was an incredibly committed Christian. He would awake before light every morning to pray and read his Bible. He would regularly quote me verses I had never met in the Bible let alone committed to memory. He is a great man.

The second story is of Emmanual. There are few Christians whose faith I have respected more. A Catholic, with a brilliant mind, he held stature and integrity beyond most. As a student at university and a Tutsi, he was a key player both academically and in the Christian Union. When the war broke out, the university campus seemed a concentrated, intensified microcosm of the problems of the country. Killings were rampant as students turned on one another. Emmanual was one of the few who held firm. He refused to break friendship with his Hutu colleagues. Despite pressure and threats from others, and whilst his own family members were being killed in other parts of the country, he kept his stance, taking the risk of hiding Hutu friends in his room. Throughout it all, he clung to what he knew was right. He knew the Bible taught him that all men were created equal and he stayed focused on the Word, obeyed it and maintained his faith whilst those round him lost theirs. He remained with steady temperament and maintained cross-tribal friendships no matter what the situation or cost.

These two stories are also typical of Burundi and hint at the glimmering shadow of God at work amidst the madness of fighting and war.

Burundi Fighting

It would be easy to come out of such a year and speak disproportionately of the violence and not enough of the beauty of the place or the people. The majority of the time in a war zone is inaction and Burundi was often relatively calm. With that proviso it has to be said it was a fierce and barbaric war. We were occasionally close enough to hear or see it.

I was aware, during certain intense periods of fighting, how my stress level rose considerably. Multiply that by 200 and I guess that would be the stress many Burundians suffered. For we were rarely the target of the violence, nor were our relatives or loved ones, and we were often living in safer areas of town.

The morning after a night of particularly heavy gun and mortar fire, we would meet our staff and instantly see the stress written on their faces. It put our own tiredness into perspective. They recounted a night of fleeing, lying low in ditches, being separated from loved ones and were evidently terrified. Coming to work was a chance to escape and for a while many of them brought their families to live in our gardens as there were few other places they felt safe.

In 1999 the UN termed Burundi the most dangerous country in the world. I wrote the following in a letter whilst sitting in the capital:

Politically things have declined. Fighting has continued to increase, there have been many recent attacks on the road between here and Kayanza (where we work) so we are now using the plane. Last Thursday thirty-eight people were reported to have been killed in one attack.

In Bujumbura, gun battles are frequently heard. One night we were forced to stay with friends because it was too dangerous to leave as machine guns and mortar fire were heard nearby. Another night it was alarmingly loud and sounded like it could have been on streets either side of our house. At times it gets to the stage where you mistake every clunk, clink and little bang as gunfire.

Last Tuesday [12 October 1999], a UN envoy was ambushed, people were lined up against a wall and two UN personnel were shot dead, including a logistician. The others managed to escape after fleeing for over ninety minutes. This news shocked us all, not since 1996 had an expat been shot, not to mention deliberately targeted. As a result, the UN is on its highest security alert; it has evacuated all non-essential staff. Many other NGOs have evacuated their teams from the countryside.

In response to this heightened fighting, the military have decided to try and flush out all the rebels from Bujumubura. Their method: shift the entire population of the Bujumbura rural suburbs into displacement camps. I am not sure whether it will help win the war effort in the long term but in the short term, about 300,000 people have been forced to live in camps, with no water, little food, no shelter from the rains and hot sun, no latrines, nothing. Is there anywhere else in the world where so many are living with so little? English sheep are better off.

Undoubtedly one of the most dangerous roads in Burundi was the RW1. This road was also the main artery of Burundi running north from the capital, into Rwanda, then Uganda, then Kenya before the Indian Ocean. It was also the road that linked the capital to our project base at Kayanza. The death rate on that road was extraordinarily high. Drivers, passengers and cyclists were frequently injured or died after hurtling down from the mountains; near misses on our own journeys seemed to happen with alarming frequency. The road was also perfect rebel territory, lots of bends, high cliffs, lots of bushes – very easy to get a good view of the road and not be seen, very easy to shoot and then disappear. On average I guess there was an attack on that road once a week. When the rebels attacked they were ruthless, shooting dead entire bus loads. A couple of minutes is all it took and then back into the bush, out of view, with thirteen families left to grieve and bury their dead.

The war in Burundi was very different from wars in other countries. Unlike Sudan the rebels did not control or 'capture' towns. There were no front lines. They were everywhere and they were nowhere. You had no idea where they were or who they were. They could attack you in the evening and in the morning wake up 30 kilometres away. It was this that made them and the country so dangerous.

At the time it was very hard to conceive of peace ever coming to that tiny land yet there is now a peace accord. As one reflects back on where Burundi was, it is amazing to see how far it has travelled. No doubt it still has a long way to go, but it would be interesting to compare the statistics of Burundians killed with a 'high-profile' conflict such as Palestine. Palestine receives far more coverage than Burundi ever has, but I suspect not as many deaths. Even in 1999 I remember reading newspaper reports of the Middle East and the Gaza strip – they felt very mild compared to Burundi. A fragile peace has arrived in Burundi; maybe that can give us encouragement as we seek hope for other conflicts.

Christmas 1999

Christmas, away from family, is a time you brace yourself for home sickness, a time to psych yourself up and come out determined to have a great time. Christmas 1999 was the brainchild of Dieudonne[3], a talented young Christian Burundian, well-educated and smart who had decided to start his own 'charity' from nothing. With no money and forsaking the prospects of a business career or further study overseas he remained in Bujumbura and began sdedicating his life to the ministry of street kids. Some of his story is included as a footnote...it's worth a read.

He befriended Si Guillebaud (a young English missionary living in Burundi), who, with characteristic enthusiasm, threw his weight behind the idea. Soon they had a number of other NGO workers and friends donating money and vehicles toward the scheme.

Before it kicked off, I went to Jabbe church. The church is a ramshackle building, made from rusted corrugated iron and wooden poles. The inside was crammed to overflowing with people and worship. One of my abiding memories of Burundi is singing in that church. Hundreds of people lifting their voices to the Lord in a tight space would move anyone. The songs were neither in English nor French but, oblivious to what I should sing, I would join in anyway and add my out-of-tune voice to the throng. Somehow, not knowing the words frees you from their framework; worship becomes more sensual, more about your spirit and less about your mind.

I went from church to home, pulled on some beach clothes and got the pick-up to where we were meeting the street kids. Other vehicles soon arrived and we overloaded the pick-ups with kids and took them to the shore of Lake Tanganika. We were soon up to our necks in children – play-fighting, tickling, scrambling for tennis balls, diving into the soft sand, splashing around in the water. Kids have such a capacity for unreserved laughter and fun. The more courageous ventured excitedly into the water, gleefully splashing about, their scrawny limbs and skinny bodies flailing everywhere, eager to be thrown in deeper. Kids arose from the water, snotty nosed, lips grinning, teeth shining and water twinkling and sparkling off their black skin, eager to be thrown in again. Unashamed in delight, exhilarated by the experience, eager to get as much of the games whilst they lasted, their lack of inhibitions helped us all relax and forget our reserve.

A huge meal was prepared, we all sat down (144 street kids), boys and men alike and tucked in, gobbling away to our hearts' delight. After the meal, Dieudonne, the inspiration and organizer of the day, stood up and gave thanks. With displacement camps clearly visible on the hills behind him, he talked about the gifts we had received, but spoke most about the gift God gave the world, commemorated each year, in every country on Christmas Day.

We hoped we had been a part of giving something special to the children. We arrived back as dark was setting in, cracked open a beer, collapsed into a sofa, shattered but rejoicing in the day having experienced what Christmas was all about; realizing afresh that it is in giving that one receives.

Bujumbura, a small African capital besieged by war – thank you for a great Christmas.

A Trip through Rwanda

There are no devils left in Hell. They are all in Rwanda.[4]

The border is marked by a meandering river, snaking its way through a narrow valley. The bridge crossing the river is no man's land. To the north lies Rwanda and to the south Burundi. Our approach from the south was a steep, windy descent; the first few miles into Rwanda were a steep, windy ascent.

Finding books on Rwanda is much easier than on Burundi. I had read far more on Rwanda and so in many ways felt I understood it better. Theirs was also an easier situation to understand. The war had ended five years before I arrived and had essentially boiled down to two tribes (Hutu and Tutsi) represented by two political factions (Interhamwe and Rwandan Patriotic Front) who fought in the most brutal terms. In April 1994 the Hutu president was flying into Kigali when his plane was shot out of the sky. The country burst into a frenzy of killing and Hutu propaganda called upon fellow Hutu to kill anything remotely Tutsi or supporting a Tutsi. In less than three months, between 800,000 and 1,000,000 people, predominantly Tutsi, were killed. Neighbour turned upon neighbour, family member upon family member. It was the fastest genocide ever. The killings were more 'efficient' even than the German genocide of the Jews in the Second World War and yet a very high proportion of the deaths were from machete attacks.[5] When Desmond Tutu visited a few months later he was so struck by the sight of skulls that still had machetes and daggers embedded in them that he wrote: 'I couldn't pray. I could only weep.'[6]

I was intrigued by the country and how it and the people were coping only five years after the terrible genocide. The opportunity to visit came when Si Guillebaud suggested I accompany him on a drive through the country to a retreat in south-west Uganda.[7]

You cannot enter a country with such a dreadful recent history without it being permanently on your mind. 'Perfect ambushing country' was one of Simon's first observations: lots of blind turns, high cliffs – plenty of vantage points for would-be killers who could easily shoot and then vanish into the bush. Both Si and I were sharing the slight tension.

Simon comes from a family with over four generations connected with Central Africa. He is an accomplished musician, a brilliant rackets player, a fluent linguist and orator. He has an inspiring and vivid faith and our humours seemed to match such that we have remained close friends ever since. His great grandfather was the first missionary to Central Africa and settled in Burundi. His grandfather and grandmother also settled in Rwanda. His grandfather translated the Bible into Kinyarwandan (the Rwandan language) which mirrored his sister who translated the Bible into Kirundi in Burundi. Simon's aunt Meg now lives in Rwanda, training pastors, and now Simon, following a dramatic calling, represents the fourth generation of Guillebauds. So the country held not only the fascination of the recent past and terrible history, but was also intimately interwoven with my companion's family history.

We drove through the inevitable checkpoint and into a town called Butare. Simon's grandparents had lived there and it was a town that suffered some of the highest rates of Tutsi murders. Over 100,000 people had been killed in the area. The town was now so quiet, so tranquil and – dare I say it – peaceful. The countryside exuded a sense of timelessness – where the noise of humankind was swallowed up by the blanketing calm of the valleys. Every inch of them was being used, farmers were hoeing at the land, women were carrying firewood and nursing babies. To my eyes there were people dotted everywhere; a Rwandan would say the fields looked empty. Before the genocide it was the most densely populated country in Africa. It was hard to imagine such a serene scene hosting such bloodshed and yet one could think of nothing else. Every face seemed calm, polite and at ease. And yet every eye had witnessed killing, every ear knew the tortured scream of death, every heart the pumping fear of an imminent attack. Almost every person, certainly every Tutsi, had lost a relative. Only God knows how many died. No human can live through those experiences without trauma, stress disorder, guilt, bitterness, fear, loneliness, sadness, regret. Whilst their faces seemed placid they must mask enormous pain in their hearts.

We drove through Kigali, the capital, to the mountainous region of Byumba, 40 miles north-west of Kigali, and our destination: the home of Simon's aunt Meg and 80-year-old grandmother. As we approached the town we could not escape the sight of a Burundian refugee camp – the inhabitants of which had been under tarpaulin for eight years – another vivid picture of God's beauty scarred by the inhumanity of man.[8]

Supergran, as Simon referred to her, had been in the country for forty years. She spoke the language as well as any Rwandan, and had lived through many traumas with the people. After the genocide, she was there just to listen and support the people in their suffering. Her husband had died but she was carrying on, still trying to minister and give. Now her daughter Meg was working alongside her. I was struck by the smallness of their home. Meg's study was also her bedroom and I doubt it measured more than 10 feet by 6 feet.

Meg had prepared a meal – a gorgeous lasagne. I was eye-ing up a healthy portion of seconds when a knock came at the door and someone entered, (apparently uninvited) and as an instant reflex Meg, got up, greeted him, set him a place at the table and dished him out the remainder of the meal. 'Sorry', she said to me, probably sensing my dis-appointment, 'but culturally it is utterly unacceptable to do anything else'. There seemed to be a constant stream of such random visitors; every one of them was listened to and made to feel at home. The fact they spoke not a word of English was turned in to an advantage. On one occa-sion, as Supergran went to answer the door, she shouted behind her: 'Meg, it's that nutter again'.

It was estimated that the district of Byumba contained 30,000 widows. One of them was Edita, a friend of the Guillebaud family who had grown up with Meg as a best friend. Meg left Rwanda and was educated in England. Edita stayed and married. During the genocide, her hus-band was killed and she fled with her children to the Zairian border. She took only what she could carry and hid all her money in her bra. At the inevitable checkpoint, she denied having money. When they found it, they raped her. Unlike many that was all they did and she made it alive to the refugee camps – a 'lucky' one. She was now back living in her former home area. Amazingly she has tracked down the man that raped her, visited him in jail and told him that by the grace of God she had forgiven him.

We were to leave the next day for Uganda, but were asked to speak at the morning service. It was a weekday and so the service was at 6.00 a.m. It doesn't matter which culture you are from – getting up before the sun for a service is very difficult. Cold as it was in the *Gorillas in the Mist*-type mountains, with the fog still blanketing the valleys, we trudged up the hill and made it there on time. Out came a few drums and we began to warm up; our chattering teeth turned to chanting and our shivering to singing. I was sitting at the front and so could see everyone's faces. Perhaps it was thirty people, maybe more, crammed into a small room, dancing and singing from the bottom of their lungs. As I looked at the room at least three quarters were women and it quickly occurred to me why this was: It had nothing to do with men not wanting to get up; this was simply a good demographic sampling of the local population. Women outnumbered men. Once again all their suffering, all their grief came flooding back to me. Whilst I thought of their trials – full of pain I could never comprehend – I looked at their faces: moving to the beat of the drums, singing with all their hearts, praising the Lord, worshipping with gusto, meditating on the words; they were an exhibition of joy. Rarely or never have I been so moved by worship. Unable to speak their language, unable to understand a word of their songs I joined in with all my heart, I sang with all I had, tears welling large in my eyes. There was an inexpressible beauty in that service. Their singing and evident love of the Lord, so vividly imprinted on their faces, makes it unquestionably memorable. When it came for me to speak, utterly out of my depth, I chose words from Romans 12:12,21: 'Be faithful in prayer, patient in affliction, and joyful in hope.... Do not be overcome by evil, but overcome evil with good.' I had selected the verses the night before but that morning I realized I was preaching to the converted. It seemed to sum up all that they already were.

Notes

1. A term used to describe a family of pastoralist tribal groups.
2. From Keith Richburg, *Out of America*, Thomson Learning, 1988, page 117. In another passage he writes: 'This is what I find the most difficult to accept and comprehend. It's not the death itself, although that is bad enough. It's the anonymity of death in Africa, the anonymity of mass death. Does anyone care about their names? Does anyone at least try to count them, to record the fact that a human being has passed away from the earth and someone may be searching for him? Or is life so tenuous here that death scarcely matters?' I have subsequently read accounts of wars in the Balkans and Vietnam and would argue that anonymity generally accompanies war. This is not a uniquely 'African' phenomenon.
3. Dieudonne is vividly described in a passage from a prayer letter by Simon Guillebaud: 'It was Christmas Day 1993 when it all started. His father had just been thrown still alive into a pit and then covered over. Dieudonne felt terribly alone and destitute, with seemingly nobody and nothing in the world. But then he walked past some street children, and realized that he had $5 more than them at least. So he bought some sodas and shared the message of Christmas with them. Slowly but surely things have grown in the intervening years, and he now has sixty four children in his care. Last year he was able to return to the scene of his father's murder and preach about forgiveness and reconciliation, and he showed us a photo of him with one of the group responsible for killing his father. He also spoke of a day when they were all going hungry as a group, and as they prayed they asked the Lord to provide not just someone's scraps for them. Rather in faith they asked for the Lord to provide them with an amazing meal. At that very moment elsewhere in the capital, I was leaving an embassy function, and there was tray after tray of delicacies, all of which were to be thrown away. So I asked if I could take them for the street children, and a few minutes later arrived at New Generation's office to hand over the Ambassador for Britain's food to these cute little hungry faith-filled ambassadors for Christ!

   Through the years these little urchins have constantly seen the Lord answer their heartfelt pleas: "Give us today our daily bread"; and that is how Dieudonne wants to continue.'
4. A missionary – quoted in *Time* magazine 16 May 1994 (also quoted in Keith Richburg, *Out of America*, Thomson Learning, 1988).
5. Some of the best books to read more on this subject include: Philip Gourevitch, *We wish to inform you that tomorrow we will be killed with our families*, Picador, 2000; Lesley Bilinda, *The Colour of Darkness*, Hodder & Stoughton, 1996; and Meg Guillebaud, *Rwanda: The Land God Forgot?*, Monarch Books, 2002.
6. Desmond Tutu, *God Has a Dream*, Rider & Co., 2005, page 12.
7. Simon had just received a death threat and so appreciated a break.

8. Keith Richburg writes about the district of Byumba in his book *Out of America*, page 97: 'A man named Amiable Kaberuka is there lying on a cot in a makeshift rebel field hospital. He might be considered lucky, since luck is a relative term here; he survived with only a gunshot in the shoulder. The Hutu militia entered the school building where he and thousands of others had taken refuge. The attackers told Kaberuka that he must die because he was a Tutsi, and then they used machetes and pangas to hack and club to death his wife and three of his four children. Kaberuka they simply shot, then left him for dead amid the pile of corpses.' He gives two other very similar examples and then writes: 'Shocking? Yes. Disgusting. Impossible to read without flinching, wanting to turn the page. But this is just a small sampling of it, a few random snapshots, individual faces and stories lifted from the entire grotesque tapestry.'

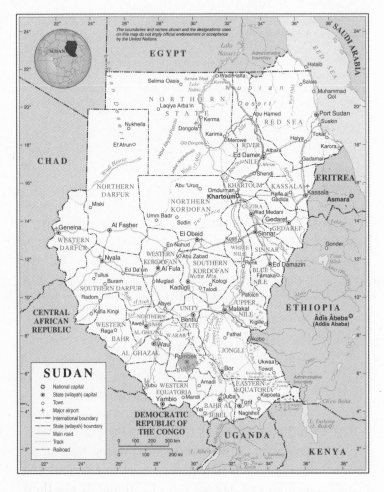

Population	41,236,378	Religion (2006 estimate)	70% Muslim, 5% Christian, 25% indigenous
Population Growth	2.55%	Language	Arabic
Prevalence of HIV	2.3%	Literacy	61%
People Living with HIV/AIDS	400,000	Life Expectancy	58

CHAPTER THREE

From Burundi to
Southern Sudan

I left Burundi in April 1999. Returning home has been the hardest aspect of relief work. Not so much because of the culture shock, though this probably has a subtle effect, more the not knowing what you are going to do next.

I looked at other options but for some reason I could find nothing that gave me 'peace'. I was not sleeping well at night and in the end called up Tearfund and asked to be considered for another assignment. The main reason I had not done so earlier was because I didn't want to be away from England, home and family. I came to see this as an insufficient reason for not following a call God might have on my life.

I ended up leading a Tearfund 'Transform' team to Kenya for the summer and a few weeks later I was in employment again, this time in Southern Sudan.

My first week in Sudan was awesome. John Baryona was the main man there, and was showing me the ropes. Within a few days he was calling me young man and I retorted with the phrase Old Man (something he took as a compliment). To this day we still affectionately use these names and remain close. John is someone I respect and love enormously. Born and bred in Sudan he has remained steadfastly loyal to the country. While many of his contemporaries have sought better lives in Kenya or the West, John has remained, often boasting: 'Peace will find me in Sudan'[1]. He was educated locally and as a first-born worked hard to ensure his brothers also got through school. He was refused his graduation and degree from Khartoum unless he joined the Government army. Doing so meant fighting against southerners, something he refused to do and so after four years of study and having passed all his exams he left without a degree. When I arrived he was working for Tearfund as their chief agriculturalist.

He picked me up from the plane and graciously introduced me to all the right people and did it all with a huge, irrepressible smile and *joie de vivre*. John is a complete extrovert and seemed to know everyone in the town. Walking down the muddy roads of Rumbek, our conversations barely got beyond the first comma because just as we got to that stage, John would be greeted by someone with whom we would have to stop and talk. It seemed to matter not whether they were prince or pauper, regal or rogue, John knew them all and treated them with the same humour and smile. One lady sticks out in my memory: she was selling groundnuts by the side of the road. Every time we greeted her in Dinka she giggled delightedly. Four years later when I visited the compound, she was still there and would still giggle and greet me with the same enthusiasm she had done over 100 times before. She was also unquestionably fat: not chubby, simply fat. Dinkas are not fat people, they are tall and lean, many have been regularly racked by hunger. In my time in Sudan I only met one other fat Dinka. His name was Dut. He had many wives and over forty children. I learnt many months later that the fat lady selling peanuts was actually the daughter of the fat man called Dut. Clearly the reason for her obesity is not just as simple as eating too many groundnut sandwiches. Fatness can be genetic.

John and I had two projects to work on and we got right into them on that first week. There was an agriculture project nearing completion and a road clearance project that needed starting.

The excitement of being with John, looking around my new home and meeting the other NGOs made it a great first week. Perhaps it was best capped by John's encounter with a stranger entering our compound: The young man was about 6 feet 6 inches tall, the shape of a prop forward with a skull as large as a beach ball. John is late-middle-aged, less than 6 feet tall and wiry. He greeted the giant with boundless enthusiasm by challenging him there and then to a wrestling match. Welcome to Southern Sudan!

Southern Sudan: The First Time

Southern Sudan switches from swelteringly hot and dry for seven months of the year to a muddy wetland in the rainy season; whether in the dry or wet season one wonders how people survive in such extreme conditions. The predominant vegetation is savannah so the ground is mainly covered in bush, high grass or acacia trees; it is also monotonously flat. The combination of vegetation and topography means you never get a view more than 200 metres and every view is the same. The sky is vast and all-surrounding in a way it never is in the UK, where buildings, hills or clouds always diminish its size. I never realized how much a view lifts your spirits, nor how lonely and oppressively small the sky can make you feel until I lived in Southern Sudan. The Nile runs through the eastern side of the country. The rest of the land is mazed with dry rivers resembling a network of lazy, flaccid snakes curled over the countryside.

The size of western Europe, with around 8 million people, Southern Sudan has been fighting the North the majority of the time since independence in 1956 with eleven years of relative peace from 1972 to 1983. By 2000, when I arrived, the southern rebels had managed to 'liberate' (as they termed it) most of the south. The Government of Sudan maintained control of a number of key towns such as Juba, Wau and Malakal which they kept heavily garrisoned. Every now and then the rebel armies mounted an attack on one, occasionally they were successful, but mostly they failed to the cost of many lives. The Government defended the towns with armies, populated with both northerners and southerners[2], they also gave 'logistical support' (weapons) to many southern militias in an attempt to divide and rule. The Government's defence was regularly buttressed by bombings from Antenov planes (Russian-built bombers) and helicopter gunship attacks. The air attacks occasionally hit military targets, but often would land near major markets, resulting in civilian deaths or casualties. The major rebel group fighting the north was the Sudan People's Liberation Army/Movement (SPLA/M), which has fought with some success over the years against the Government. There are other rebel factions and at times the SPLA has fought against those as well. In 2000 the war seemed stuck in a stalemate: neither side was able to win or lose and there was very little progress, if any, being made at the peace negotiations; the future from every angle seemed bleak.

While the southern Sudanese cultures are developed and distinct, seen through a Western lens (and crippled by war) they might be termed 'undeveloped'. There are over 170 different tribes and languages in the south, the largest being the Dinka tribe who also predominated in Rumbek where I was based. The Dinkas are nothing if not fiercely proud people. This may, in part, be related to their height. At 6 foot 1 I would often be a head shorter than them. Being with a group of Dinkas is totally bizarre: old withered men towered over me, teenagers with tiny heads and squeaky voices or women old and young would eyeball me. Their height and lengthy limbs make them very suited to walking long distances and wading across the swamps of Sudan; maybe it also contributes to their apparent self-confidence. They do not seem to suffer inferiority to any man and are apparently happy to stand up to anyone. In other cultures white skin can make it easier to earn acceptance. I never felt this to be the case with the Dinkas. I almost always had to work hard to earn their respect.

The Dinka culture was as far removed from my English one as it is possible to imagine. As nomadic agro-pastoralists, the people depend mainly on cows as a food source supplemented with arable farming. In the dry season men drive their cattle to far grazing locations called the 'toic'. As the rains return the cattle move back to the higher lands as the lowlands become too swampy[3].

It is hard if not impossible for the Western mind to grasp how greatly the Dinkas prize their cows. To rape someone's daughter is a heinous offence in any culture;

with the Dinkas I sometimes wondered whether stealing a cow was worse. Cows seem the hub to so much of their culture and practices: they are their wealth, their idols, they hold spiritual significance, their urine is used for medicinal purposes, Dinka dances are based around them, Dinka names are related to cows. I have heard stories of people prepared to lose their life to revenge the theft or death of a cow. A man will often invest in a cow instead of developing his own house. For a man to obtain a wife he needs to buy someone's daughter; cows are always the currency. The negotiations are long and complicated and both families become involved with intricate loaning systems. A man may have as many wives as he can afford; the more wives he has the richer he becomes. Each wife will bear him children and children also represent wealth: the boys can herd and manage the cows, whilst the girls can be reared and sold for more cows, and so the cyclical nature of cow wealth continues.

Maintaining your ancestral heritage also ranks as important. Every man must expand his ancestral line. The more children named after the man the better. If a male dies without children, be he a three-day-old infant or a 30-year-old man, then it is the responsibility of his nearest male relative to have children on his behalf by marrying for him. The offspring from that marriage will be assigned legally and ancestrally to the deceased male, not the biological father. Equally if a man dies before his wife conceives it will be the responsibility of his brother to ensure there are children produced in that marriage; the children will carry the name and ancestry of the dead relative as if he was their actual father. Often an old man will marry and ask one of his grown sons (born to another wife) to help his new wife conceive. The children from his son's sperm will grow up with their biological grandfather as their legal father; they may never know who their biological father is. It is a fascinating if confusing culture, I have only described a tiny part of it without doing the nuances justice. Many a conversation with Dinkas is taken up discussing cows, wives and children, often when introduced to someone's relative they will explain that he is 'their father's brother'. I learnt not to delve for a further clarification[4].

Sudan was also a very isolated place to work. Roads were poor or non-existent (I have never seen tarmac in southern Sudan), and many supplies were flown in. There were no telephones: the only form of communication with the outside world was on an HF radio, and letters could only be received when the plane landed. During the rainy season this was not always possible as the airstrip often became wet and 'unlandable'. There was no running water, toilets were a hole in the ground, accommodation was a mud hut with thatch and electricity was supplied through solar panels. It inevitably felt remote.

In 1998, a combination of factors combined to result in a famine with thousands dying, and saw the rise of a massive relief effort to save the lives of many starving. The main reasons for famine were repeated attacks by an SPLA commander on a government-held town called Wau in the heart of Bhar El Ghazel. During these attacks and reprisal attacks thousands of people were displaced. They fled to areas where food reserves were already depleted by two bad harvests, their arrival put still further pressure on limited food. On top of this, the Government, anxious not to lose Wau, fought back hard and wanted complete control of the air. They placed a ban on all aid flights into the area, and so no food could be flown in. The flight ban was occasionally lifted but only in one or two locations which allowed food to be dropped in those areas. When the hungry population heard of this, they would walk there, sometimes for days, only to find the food available was too little for the needs of the population which had swelled enormously with their influx. They then moved onto another location in the hope that food might become available there.

The famine hit headline news; graphic pictures of skin-and-bone children and adults were on TV screens the world over. Tearfund launched an appeal and established feeding programmes. By the time I arrived in Rumbek, they had stopped feeding and were concentrating on agriculture and longer-term projects.

To the Ends of the Earth (Acts 1:8)

'We just want to go home, we are fed up of living on a land which is not our own.'

What struck me most about these chiefs, who had now lived for more than eight years in a displacement camp, was their dignity. The above reply came during a meeting, after they were asked why they were prepared to give so much to clear the road – a project we were about to embark on.

That day I fell in love with the people of Maper. I was inspired by these dignified, elderly gentlemen who had been through so much. Their words motivated and continued to encourage me throughout the project. Eight years previously they had fled their home area after inter-tribal fighting. The road leading to their area was now completely overgrown; clearing it meant they could return and that supplies, trade and NGOs could support them.

Clearing the road was daunting. It was 120 kilometres long and entirely covered in trees, bush and shrub. To complete the task we had 150 machetes, some locally manufactured axes, and the World Food Programme had agreed to give us food for the workers.

The road crossed a variety of different Dinka clans and subclans. Each subclan was responsible for a different stretch of the road. Each had a different chief with a different set of men to clear. The men were not always that enthusiastic. You can ask people to clear the road, but if they do not want to then you are stuck. They are not contracted to work and if they wake up one morning and decide to drive their cattle and family 50 miles away then you have to find someone else.

I was on that road many days a week. If the men had done a lot of road clearance, my spirits lifted enormously; if they had done nothing, I became disheartened and occasionally doubted it would ever be possible to complete.

Over the weeks, however, the road progressed: A journey that once took three hours now took less than one. We saw two villages Ameth and Malek, 30 kilometres and 45 kilometres along the road respectively, resettled and repopulated. The first time I arrived in Ameth and Malek, nothing was there but tall grass and an abandoned water pump, and then weeks later we would drive through it and see it teeming with families settled with their children, animals and new homes. We were guaranteed warm milk, direct from an udder, any time we passed through.

The toughest but best day was towards Christmas. I think it was the turning point of the project. Some chiefs from Maper, in an effort to mobilize their population, had decided to camp out on the road. We had driven them about 50 kilometres from Rumbek where they stayed, in the bush, to try to encourage their men to follow. They heard a rumour that some of their men had started clearing the road about 20 kilometres north. It was our job to find and bring them food.

The chiefs assured us we would find the men this time (we had tried and failed twice before). After about twenty minutes the pick-up hit a pot hole and the leaf-spring snapped. The vehicle could go no further. We waited for the second vehicle which took another twenty minutes. There were major concerns, not least from the driver, about loading the vehicle with eight people and half a metric ton of food, in order to follow a guide who, for all we knew, was a charlatan, into the tall grass. We either had to trust him or turn back.

We were driving at walking pace. Our guide was a tall man, but the grass was taller than him. Every now and again, he would stop to climb an ant hill, or stand on our vehicle. I occasionally got up there with him and he would point at some trees in the distance, but every tree looked the same. It felt like we were following a Crocodile Dundee, marching through the bush, guided by some bearings that were completely invisible to the rest of us. We had no idea whether he was a fraud, nor whether he could find the way back. The vehicle's radiator began overheating, clogged up by the grass. We poured our water on it, but still it continued to overheat. After three hours we had gone 13 kilometres and just poured our last water into an overheating engine. I had no idea if we would find the place we were looking for, nor whether we could find our way back. The sun was getting lower and with the vehicle playing up, we were staring at the possibility of either walking back or staying the night in the bush while the engine cooled down. The driver did not want to go on, he thought that the guide was a swindler and that the car would not make it. Soon an argument broke out – things were not going well. Then suddenly, out of nowhere, came a man with his wife and two small children, who told us there was a pond about 2 kilometres away.

What should we do now? Should we take their word for it and risk going further into the bush without water? Should we turn back and limp home with a failed mission where at least we know that water will be available about 30 kilometres away? I had no idea what we should do, my mind was completely afuzz. With hindsight the obvious option was to go for the nearest water point, but at the time people were very sceptical that was true. Thankfully, we pressed on and in the middle of this barren, dry, brown wilderness we found a waterhole. The driver could cool the engine and fill up the water reserves whilst we walked on and found the guys clearing the road. Five of them had based themselves there, but they said they had run out of food and were planning on leaving the next day if none arrived. We looked at what they had cleared and saw a good 2 kilometres of beautifully cleared grass, burnt down to the roots. Whilst not a lot in itself, it was an encouraging sight.

We left them food and lots of hearty thanks before

beginning our journey back, our spirits markedly higher. We had achieved our aims, we came through arguments and breakdowns and were now returning. The chiefs were delighted to see us and hear our good news. They offered us something to drink before we set off into the night. We got to Rumbek after 9.00 p.m., having left at 6.00 a.m. that morning.

The atmosphere on the journey back reminded me of a bus full of rugby lads returning victorious from a big game. Dinka songs were sung, crude jokes were cracked and we took enormous pleasure in repeatedly reversing over a deadly snake. The crude jokes were akin to those heard in any sports team but with an African slant: 'How do snakes do it?' someone enquired. 'The same way as lizards,' came the triumphant reply (I was none the wiser). Dinkas often get their Ps and Fs muddled up and so I chuckled as another informed us that 'A duck has a very large fenis'.

I am not someone particularly in tune with the 'spirit's prompting' or that often talks of the spiritual world. But on this project and subsequent ones working in Maper, I felt a strong spiritual sense that we were part of something greater. The project itself was about far more than just clearing the road, it was about returning displaced people to their homelands; but I had a kind of intuitive feeling that we were influencing a spiritual realm somehow. When I later lived in Maper, a deserted town that had seen massive misery and bloodshed, I often felt a 'heavy' spiritual presence. Don't ask me how I felt it, but it did feel tangible. At such times the verse I would turn to, either in my mind or physically in my Bible, read 'The one who is in you is greater than the one who is in the world' (1 John

4:4). For some reason I needed to constantly remind myself of this truth during those months.

The day I just described was the turning point of the whole road project. Had we failed, I believe people would have lost heart, given up and stopped working. The fact that we succeeded somehow gave people a hope and optimism; like a team that get's on a winning roll, we always felt we were going to succeed from then on. It sounds trite, but looking back, I see the Lord's hand on that day, guiding us and getting us through: when the argument was at its most intense, we suddenly met some people (the only sign of life after 13 kilometres) who pointed us to the pond; when we were unsure whether we should return home or carry on, it feels as though the Lord was in the decision to press on. Arguments, irrational thoughts and cars breaking down could be just that, and maybe they were, but maybe they were part of something greater. As I remember that day now, somehow the killing of the snake seems more than just a bit of laddish fun; it now seems a symbolic sign of victory.

From then on the road project had many difficult days and over 70 kilometres to clear. There were times when we had to camp out overnight, times when the vehicles broke down, times when a water point stopped working and we were forced to truck out a metric ton of water; but generally the work was a lot smoother and by February 2001, 120 kilometres of road had been cleared to Maper. The first time I arrived in Maper, and waded through the long grass and ruined buildings, it truly felt like we had arrived at the end of the earth. Hacking away at some stubborn tree trunks on the final section of the road was a hardy, ragtag, rustic gaggle of men. Nervously, I went to greet them; as I arrived, they dropped tools and offered to pray for me. Later on I attended church (under a tree) with them.

I was incredibly proud to have been a tiny part of the project which at times had felt almost impossible. But the road in itself was only the first rung in the ladder of helping people return to their ancestral lands. The second rung was to be our next project.

Working in Maper

Following the completion of the road, we tried to help people return and resettle in Maper (see section below). We also became involved in a child soldiers demobilization project (see page 64). I took a short break before it all began and on the plane back read the passage below from Isaiah 61. I was then sent a similar passage from Isaiah 55 by a friend. They were a tremendous encouragement to me and felt uncannily apt for the work we were about to do. I have, many times, turned and drawn inspiration from them and other such passages in Isaiah. Such verses seem to define most clearly the heart of Tearfund and the work it does.

> He has sent me to bind up the brokenhearted, to proclaim freedom for the captives and release from darkness for the prisoners, to proclaim the year of the Lord's favour...to comfort all who mourn, and provide for those who grieve in Zion – to bestow on them a crown of beauty instead of ashes, the oil of gladness instead of mourning, and a garment of praise instead

of a spirit of despair.... They will rebuild the ancient ruins and restore the places...that have been devastated for generations.   (Isaiah 61:1– 4)

Is this not the kind of fasting I have chosen: to loose the chains of injustice...to set the oppressed free and break every yoke? Is it not to share your food with the hungry and to provide the poor wanderer with shelter – when you see the naked, to clothe him, and not to turn away from your own flesh and blood?

If you spend yourselves on behalf of the hungry and satisfy the needs of the oppressed... The Lord will guide you always; he will satisfy your needs in a sun-scorched land... Your people will rebuild the ancient ruins and will raise up the age-old foundations.

(Isaiah 58:6–7,10–12)

Projects in Maper

There were three major reasons for working in Maper. The first was to help families return and resettle. (One way we did that was, in the absence of any clean water, to provide five water points for the area. UNICEF contracted a driller and we supported them logistically to drill to the water table 80 metres below the surface. This could then be hand-pumped to the surface by anyone that wanted it). The second reason was to try to support the Wunlit peace deal signed between the Dinka and Nuer tribes who had fought throughout much of the 1990s, resulting in thousands dead including many from Maper (which was on the border between the tribes). The final purpose for being in Maper was to support families fleeing fighting from a region to the north called Western Upper Nile.

Within days of our arrival they started to appear – 10 kilometres north we met dozens of Nuer who had recently fled attacks. Never had I seen such raw shock and trauma written so clearly on people's faces. Clothes were torn, eyes were bloodshot, hands were still shaking and one baby in particular was very severely malnourished. They recounted how their homes had been attacked and burnt and they had run for their lives. We were 130 kilometres from the nearest health centre or NGO: these displaced people only had Tearfund and the fledgling returning Dinka community to help them. The Dinkas provided them with land, social support, and crucially, given their recent history, assurances of safety. Tearfund provided basic food and household items (blankets, cooking pots, fishing lines, etc.), ensured a water point was drilled in their area, and helped the baby recover from malnutrition. It felt as though a tiny part of the vision was being realised.

In subsequent months I found myself meeting other people who had fled fighting in the north. On one occasion I interviewed an old, frail lady accompanied by her blind and equally delicate husband. The difference between her and the husband is that she was at least wearing one item of clothing. The discussion wasn't easy: it was the middle of the day, the sun was up, they had very soft voices and trying to work out their history through a translator was not straightforward, their body odour could also have been better. So whilst I was struggling to think up vaguely intelligent questions, the one which kept recurring in my mind was whether they thought it hygienic to allow the man's 'middle-stump' to waggle around in the dirt.

To help the permanent resettlement of the communities, UNICEF urged us to build schools. The idea was to build them almost entirely from local materials and labour. In most parts of the world, you can quite easily find labourers and brickies. Usually they are regarded as fairly low skill labour. Not so in Maper. As they told us in repeated meetings, 'We know nothing about buildings, bricks or cement, we know only about cows and cattle.' Then finally, in a meeting, a man put up his hand and said he knew how to make mud bricks. It felt as though we had met Picasso.

There were a few other people who moved back with knowledge in building and we relied on them and a few hired artisans to construct the buildings. The schools were food-for-work projects with all the accompanying frustrations.

Soon, however, the foundations were dug, mud bricks were laid, the walls were plastered with local sand and cement; and zinc sheets were bought for the roof. The motivated communities built three schools (each with two classrooms) and two health clinics (with one room) in four months. The last I heard the schools were still being used.

The schools and water points themselves were great, but they signified far more than that. They encouraged people to return to the area, they signalled that people (and God) cared about them. The people had fled following successive raids from the Nuer and now, following a peace process, families from both tribes were living side by side. Both helped build and use the schools. I, along with some chiefs, spoke at meetings on the value of forgiveness.

Someone approached me after one such meeting and told me how he had lost his mother and brothers in the fighting and asked me how I could speak about forgiveness? He probably rightly perceived that I was a naïve and innocent man, in his mid twenties, speaking on things beyond himself. I had to agree it probably wasn't right for me to speak on forgiveness – a subject that is complex and difficult. The issues between the tribes were far greater and deeper than I ever could hope to understand or relate to.

I now wonder what he understood by the word 'forgiveness'. At its most basic it means 'not seeking revenge'. It also has something to do with not being tied to bitterness and hatred. Forgiveness is a process, not a one-off action, and it can be compatible with a righteous desire for justice. All I can do now is hope and pray some of our actions and words were a positive force in the lengthy healing process required.

Child Soldiers

Forced child recruitment or conscription had long been occurring in Southern Sudan, not least by the Sudan People's Liberation Army (SPLA). Many children died on the front line as a result. Those that survived led a life away from families, schools, and all that is the 'right' of any child. Killing and the scars of battle often left them traumatised and alienated from their own humanity, struggling to return to the society from which they came.

In 2001 the UN organised a child demobilisation programme. Following discussions between SPLA commanders and UN top officials it was decided the SPLA would

Burundi

On the shores of Lake Tanganika in Burundi. Mist hovers over the capital Bujumbura, a city that was besieged by war from 1993 to 2005. During that time there were many displacement camps in the hills, where hundreds of thousands fled, forced from their homes as a result of the fighting.

Si Guillebaud and I would often head down to the lake to throw a ball around (above left). Seven years after leaving we returned for a holiday to enjoy a country now in peace (above right). We are now married with children (Lizzie Guillebaud, left, holding Zac and Rachel, right, holding our daughter Iona.)

Southern Sudan

Cows are at the centre of Sudanese culture and much of life revolves around them. The above picture shows a cattle-camp in the early morning. The smoke is caused by cow-dung, which is burnt to keep the flies away. Below, Dinka men and boys are guarding their cattle. To keep the flies away, they would smear the ash of the burnt cow dung on their face and bodies.

A 'manyatta' (small gathering of huts) in the rocky desert of Northern Kenya. It is hard to imagine a more difficult environment in which to survive.

Camel rearing is one of the main livelihoods in southern Sudan where herders would have to live off camel milk for days on end.

The Rendille women adorned themselves with a beautiful mane of beaded necklaces, headware and bracelets.

The man in the picture below is a friend of mine, his wife (second from left) is holding their baby girl to whom she gave birth five days before in the hut behind us – thankfully the birth was successful. We discussed a name for the child and settled on Naomi.

Rachel was working for Tearfund's Disaster Management Team, as a nurse. In the above shot she is sitting inside a hut and the below shot she is with some Dinka on a survey.

Just married!
19th June 2004.

We didn't live in the same country until a few months before we got married. Here we are on top of Table Mountain, in South Africa.

Sierra Leone

In the dense jungles of Sierra Leone, at a village abandoned during the war. We were trying to help refugee's return and resettle. In the above shot I am helping to build some latrines – my colleague is laughing at my ineptitude.

Khartoum & Darfur

Khartoum has to be the hottest and driest city in the world. The photograph above shows a dust storm moments before it covered the city – including the inside of our appartment – in sand. Below, a fishermen plies his trade on the river Nile.

give their soldiers under the age of 18 to the UN who would take them out of the front line and fly them to Rumbek, a relative safe haven. Every year the fighting escalates during the dry season and dwindles in the wet season. The UN intimated they had been told the exact date that the fighting in Northern Bhar El Ghazel was due to start and therefore we had a ready-made deadline to aim for. No one quite knew how many were due to come, but it was essential that camps be set up with available water, shelter and food before they arrived.

Reactions from NGOs varied: why the sudden rush now, was it a self-made emergency, what provisions were made, was this just a chance for the SPLA to get some free schooling from the UN, who would fund it, was the cost worth it, etc.

The time between this idea being hatched and the arrival of the children could not have been more than a month. UNICEF does not 'implement' programmes itself directly; it coordinates and funds others to. So whilst negotiating with commanders to release child soldiers was at the very core of what UNICEF does, running a camp was not. It was prepared to drill water, advise on camp layout, provide soap, clothes, and school books, and fly in experts in child demobilisation, but running the camps would have to be done by NGOs.

Tearfund were approached. It was agreed that one camp for demobilised child soldiers would be established in Maper. This meant a whole load of planning meetings and task force groups to ensure that when these children arrived there was something on the ground in readiness for them. Sometimes I hear a phrase on the TV or radio saying 'agencies are struggling to cope'. I now read this as a euphemism for 'bedlam and chaos'. Certainly that was how it occasionally felt as we worked hard and earnestly, but not always productively, to prepare for the child soldiers. The head of UN operations would encourage us with words like 'sometimes you have to build the tracks as the train is driving along'. Often it felt more like we were rummaging around for anything resembling a railway sleeper hours after the train had chugged past.

After a weekend of meetings with the UN and a desperate scramble to get sufficient staff we set off in a land-cruiser. We arrived in Maper, interviewed a few more people and gave almost everyone a job. The UN sent up truck loads of food, equipment and 'kits' for the children. We sorted out the 'carers' into pairs and drew up plots and latrines which would be made into huts and toilets. We had a day and a half to get ready.

The first arrived at dusk and the final of four lorries arrived well after dark. Children who had been working in the army were now suddenly disarmed, thrown into an airplane, flown to a distant land, put in a truck, driven at night along a bumpy road into the absolute heart of a wilderness...Maper. The children, packed into the back of a lorry, were more reminiscent of people arriving in Nazi concentration camps than liberated, exalted, former child soldiers, grateful for their freedom. They had left familiarity behind, many of them not older than eight or nine years of age and were now in an unknown, uninhabited, dark, savannah bush. They got off the truck, almost silently, received their rations with barely a whimper, and went off to find a bit of thornless ground on which to sleep. It was an unnatural environment – virtually all male, few mother figures or women and no relatives.

However, it was not the front line and at least they were alive.

The children had each been given a blanket, and they settled down under the stars to sleep. They drew close to one another for warmth but also for emotional comfort. Despite hundreds of children in a small area, there was quiet. The air was still and hushed; sadness seemed to roll over the camp like a coastal fog. I walked through the camp staring at these children who huddled together for reassurance. Much as these boys had fought on the front line, much as they knew the workings of a machine gun, they were still boys. My heart went out to them, I wanted to be their brother, their mother, their father. I wanted to comfort each one of them. I remembered how I had felt, leaving home aged eighteen. I remembered how painful it was being without my family and familiar surroundings. At least I could phone home. These little guys were going through these emotions ten years younger than I had, but they did not know when they would return and they had no way of hearing the comforting voice of their mother.

I was walking slowly through the camp with Gabrial. He was an amazing Dinka, the last couple of days he had been brilliant: organising everything, working incredibly hard, always smiling and always encouraging. The day's work had been done and we were chatting with the more relaxed and open manner that comes with not having to worry about the next task. We had worked hard in the past few days and mysteriously we had bonded. Nothing had been said, you couldn't quite put your finger on it, but we were now close. There are times when a genuine friendship transcends culture. Our humour, language and background were poles apart and yet as we walked through the camp I felt as close to him as a brother. I knew a bit about his background and asked him now. He opened up and explained how when Rumbek had been captured by the Government in 1987 he had walked, as a child, to Ethiopia, a dangerous journey of at least 400 miles. Once there he was a child soldier and part of the SPLA training camps. He had walked for weeks lured by the promise of good food. When he arrived he found little to eat. He hoped for education but learnt only the ABC of the gun. Separated from his family, he did not even know whether his mother or brothers were still alive. In 1991, the communist Government in Ethiopia was overthrown; the new power was not in favour of camps inside their borders and attacked them. Gabrial fled once more and this time ended up in Kenya (after another dangerous walk of over 400 kilometres) in a refugee camp where at last he received schooling before finally returning back to Rumbek. He was away from home for twelve years. He said time and again 'it was utterly miserable'. He ended his tale (similar to that shared by thousands of others) by repeating a question to me: 'Why did God allow me to spend my childhood and adolescent years away from my mother? Why couldn't I have spent those years with my mother?' I had no answer. He went on, 'Why is there war in Sudan? Is God punishing us?' Tears were in my eyes. These same questions probably lie deep within thousands of Sudanese. Maybe also many others who have suffered terribly wonder whether it is a punishment from God. I cannot remember what I said in reply, I hope I assured him that it was not a punishment from God and that God did love him. As to why God allowed him to be separated from his mother? I still do not know.

We had a few days more with the camp in Maper, then a town 40 kilometres west of us degenerated in fighting. The UN declared Maper unsafe; the camp had to close. The children were sent to another camp near Rumbek while we remained in Maper. I was extremely sad to say goodbye. Doubts remain over the efficacy and purpose of the demobilisation exercise. The children remained in Rumbek through the wet season and then were returned to their home areas, where the fighting had died down and UNICEF began investing in education infrastructure in their home area.

Notes

1. His boast proved prophetic. When the Comprehensive Peace Agreement was signed in January 2005, John was still living and working in Southern Sudan.
2. Often it is assumed that the Government armies were only filled with northerners. In fact a large number originated from the south, often coerced or heavily persuaded by the Government. For example, John Baryona was refused his degree certificate unless he joined the army for one year.
3. The words 'highlands' and 'lowlands' may be misleading – the gradient between them is virtually indiscernible but over a number of miles it does make a difference.
4. In John Briley's book *Cry Freedom* (Penguin, 1987) the author outlines an argument from Steve Biko who claims the African way of terming relatives as a 'father's brother' rather than an 'uncle' is far superior as it highlights the closeness; 'uncle' is a more distant, aloof term.

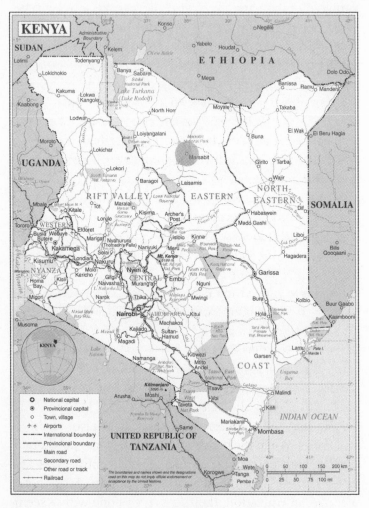

Population	34,407,817 (estimate 2006)	Religion	78% Christian, 10% Muslim, 12% other and indigenous
Population Growth	2.57%	Language	Kiswahili and English
Prevalence of HIV	6.7%	Literacy	85%
People Living with HIV/AIDS	1.2 million	Life Expectancy	48

CHAPTER FOUR

From Sudan to Northern Kenya

I loved the months in Maper but they were also very raw. In heat daily over 40°C we were showering behind a bush and burying our stools with a spade. With no fridge all water and food was warm. We were regularly dealing with the difficult local authorities and SPLA/M commanders and leaders who seemed to give us unreasonable hassle, including banning me from jogging and demanding food intended for others.

So while I loved my time in Sudan, at times towards the end of my assignment I saw my temper become short and hard to control and I believe a part of me had been 'broken down'. Certainly whatever it is that normally prevents me from losing my temper was not working. If I struggled to maintain an even disposition and balanced perspective, with all I had in my favour, it is hardly surprising that the southern Sudanese could also, at times, lose theirs. When the bombs dropped they had nowhere to hide. A high percentage would go their entire lives and never lay eyes on the sea or a mountain. Most never received an education; their future was one with a seemingly unending war, constantly depriving them of advancement and freedom. Even the most sheltered 'backward' person in Sudan knows that miles away through the long grass is a life of riches and opportunity.

They want their life to improve in the same way almost every human does. The difference is that they are trapped and imprisoned, having been born into a world of limited opportunity. If I had good reasons for being grumpy, they had better ones.

With the onset of the rainy season Maper became inaccessible and I moved to the Northern Kenyan Programme. As I boarded the plane out of Sudan at the end of my assignment, I found myself praying: 'Lord, may I never have to come back to this country'. Having arrived excited, I left shattered. My prayer, as it turns out, was not to be answered but I did not know that then.

After a break on the Kenyan coast with my sister, I returned to Nairobi and flew to Marsabit. I was met by Martha, a beautiful Kenyan woman. We got in the pick-up and drove. Marsabit, in northern Kenya, is a town on the top of a mountain. The mountain is the highest point of the highlands which rise out of the huge, wide, flat expanse that is the Chalbi desert.

There was no tarmac and the road out of Marsabit had degenerated into rivulets running across the road from one side to the other. It was not dissimilar to driving over one long corrugated iron sheet. We turned off onto a track through the rocks and headed down. The scenery was unlike any I had seen before or could have imagined. Brown, grey, and dark red granite rocks were everywhere. It was utterly dry. Nothing grew except a few sporadically scattered scrub trees.

As the road got lower so the rocks became smaller and eventually the rocks were left behind us, replaced by sand. We had driven for at least an hour to get to this point. I had noticed no sign of human dwellings. It was completely barren. We drove on, and the sand became white, then yellow. This was the classical desert seen in the photos but without sand dunes, just flat. In the distance there was something like a lake, something like evaporating water, something like gas rising from the ground. It was none of these things. It was the shimmering mirage that disappeared as you drove nearer.

Far away to our left were cliffs. I was told palm trees and springs were at the foot of the cliffs where herders would drive their cattle for water. Some communities had to walk their camels for seven days to get water, load them up and return. They then took a day's rest and began the journey again for more water.

Our road had turned to a track now, but we pressed on. Some tracks went in another direction. 'That's the road to Kargi,' someone shouted at me. We drove on for another half hour or so. Evidently now we had reached the end of the pure desert as the sand turned into white, pure white, just like a layer of snow. 'Salt,' someone shouted at me. 'After the rains, the water evaporates and leaves salt.' We drove through the salt and then into another rocky patch. Nothing surrounded us but hard black and brown rocks. Now we were crossing a couple of hills, we turned a corner and then – could this really be a settlement of people, a town? A number of houses, made from wood and hardened sand. How did anyone live here? How did they survive? What did they live on? Why are they still here?

'This is Maikona,' they said. We had arrived. We drove through the town, with me staring in disbelief. How could humans exist on this moonscape? We came over a small hill and I saw our camp. Tents, a fence and a few thorn trees; there was nothing else.

I have been to a few camps and bases that Tearfund have set up, but this was the most difficult to adjust to. No doubt about it. 'Welcome,' I heard people say. Were they being ironic? Surely they couldn't genuinely mean that?

What had I done? Why on earth had I agreed to come to this place for six months? It was summer back in Britain – I could be having so much fun. Was I genuinely off my rocker?

I have always been a good sleeper and often, when feeling low, cannot wait for the relief it brings. I went into my tent as early as was acceptable and fell asleep.

The zip on my tent had broken and when I awoke the next morning, I looked up, saw the first gentle lights of dawn and watched a caravan of camels walk past. Maybe this place wasn't so bad?

I was to have a ten-day handover. We would then 'up and move' the base to another location called Korr, where we would replicate the feeding and health education project until Christmas. During those first few days, I and a few others visited Korr, to check it out and find a base there. I was hoping it would be different and a bit nicer. The colours were different – the rock changed from a blackish brown to a yellowy brown – but essentially it was still a rocky desert with nothing there.

During the handover – I was trying to learn the ropes, pick up and understand how 'nutrition projects' worked but was also going through mental agony. The same questions kept ringing in my ears. What was I doing here? Could I get out of it? How I wished I was with my family.

The day of our move to Korr I was alone in a pick-up with the driver, Mega. We were later to become close friends but at that stage all I was thinking about was getting out of there. Our vehicle developed a problem and so the others drove on whilst we continued at about half their speed. The entire journey took us about six hours.

Whilst I let no one else on the team know, I was seriously considering resigning before I had even really begun. I spent those hours in the car contemplating my situation. I don't think I uttered a word to Mega as my mind panned through every possible scenario. I considered everything, I prayed, I begged God to give me some sort of exit. 'Yes – of course I have said I will serve you anywhere, Lord, but that was before I knew somewhere like this could possibly exist!'

For those six hours I wrestled with the Lord and the Lord won. By the time I got to Korr, the guys had already begun work on the new compound and were excited. I stepped out of the car and felt like a new man. I slept that night and woke up excited, happy in my surroundings and glad in the new day. All my worries, anxieties and fears had amazingly gone.

I spent six months in Korr and though, of course, there were times when I was lonely, missed home and found it tough, I remember it now as a special time in my life. I fell in love with Korr and the people in the area. I remember it with immense fondness and there will always be a special place in my heart for the Rendille people (the predominant tribe in the area). I returned for a holiday over two years later with Rachel (she had worked in Maikona before me). I was keen to share with her something of this special place and it was on that holiday, having been in a relationship for just over a year, that we agreed to marry...but more on that later.

As a team we would sing worship songs every night, and quite regularly someone would choose a song with a line in the chorus: 'I will follow you anywhere, Lord'. It always seemed to attract more volume than any other song. Probably, we had all gone through similar journeys.

Northern Kenya

You are almost always guaranteed a hot, wide, vast vista in northern Kenya. The colours change with the geology from white to yellow, to dark red, to many shades of brown and to black. The hills and mountains are angular and steep, with flat sandy plains below.

We were working in Marsabit district, an area larger than Wales with a population smaller than Swansea; thinly populated by a variety of tribes, predominantly the Gabra, Boran, Samburu and Rendille. All the tribes are of Cushite origin. This is a different family from the pastoral Nilotics, from which the Dinkas came, or the cultivating Bantus, from which many Burundians (the Hutus) came. The Cushites are different in appearance. Their skin colour is lighter, their features are sharp and angular and their hair somewhere between tight curls and straight. They are lean and the beauty of the women is breathtaking. It is said that Ethiopians are the best looking race in Africa; they too are Cushites. The Gabra, who lived in Maikona, wore vivid headscarves and the Rendille women in Korr (the tribe with whom we spent most of our time) wore coloured beads round their arms, their legs, crafted into a crown shape on their heads, and around their necks. Those around their neck could number as many as fifty separate necklaces, bound together into one heavy mane. This they would never or rarely take off, certainly never in public. Without it they could feel utterly naked. The men often wore their hair down to the centre of their backs, with wild sisal braided into their natural hair, usually dyed a bright red. They too would decorate their heads with brightly beaded crowns and often a flower above their temple. On their arms, across their chest, around their waist and on their ankles would be more coloured beads. They were an impressive sight.

The traditional diet of these tribes was milk, meat and blood. That was it, nothing else. The milk would be direct from the udder of a sheep, a goat, a camel or occasionally a cow. A man with a doctorate assured me that before the age of twelve nothing had passed his lips but milk; on a good day it would be from a camel. The second part of their diet was meat, eaten more rarely, but would come from the same animals. The sheep in the area were a rare desert variety: above their rump was stored a large deposit of fat. Rather like the hump on a camel, it was a reserve the sheep could burn off in times of drought. The Rendille enjoyed eating fat and would eat pure chunks of it raw, to provide the energy required for the long walks. In the traditional Rendille marriage, the groom presents the bride's family with a large slab of uncooked fat. The third part of their diet was blood, obtained by tapping the veins of an animal and often mixed with milk. Every now and then someone killed a zebra or giraffe and then a feast would ensue. In times of real hardship, women would dig out roots for cooking. The diet seemed to work: when you saw the men and women who spent their entire time herding cattle they were, almost without exception, muscular and well defined. I sometimes wonder whether Dr Atkins had studied or heard of such people groups and their diets.

Traditionally there were no towns. People lived in 'manyattas' – a collection of a dozen or more huts, each made from branches covered in sheep and goat skin. They were no taller than a man, with little space inside. These manyattas would shift wherever the livestock went, which in turn would move wherever the grazing was. The young men would tend the animals; the young women reared the children; the old women would remain in the manyattas and help while the old men would run the show. In this way the entire community could stay together and access their milk, meat and blood. Over recent decades that has been changing as settlements have grown into villages and towns. With this have come plenty of benefits but also, inevitably, an erosion of some coping mechanisms.

Two major factors lead to the growth of larger villages and towns: development and the availability of guns. Settlements developed around permanent water points, drilled or dug to new depths by outside technology which contained water the year round. Around these – often as a result of missionaries – schools, hospitals, clinics and churches were built, and so villages and towns developed.

Another driving force was the availability of the AK-47. Tribes have their rough borders where they can graze their animals, they negotiate with other tribes and broadly there are outlines of conduct they follow; but tribal conflict has always been part of their life. Skirmishes in the past involved spears and maybe bows and arrows. In recent decades the Kalashnikov has become easily accessible for a cheap price. A tribal attack from thirty men with spears would be short lived with a few injuries; a tribal attack from ten people armed with guns results in far more casualties and fatalities. Suddenly old women, mothers and children become increasingly vulnerable. No community can survive if their children and women are killed and so increasingly they are encouraged to settle in the towns while it is the men who remain in the distant manyattas with most of the animals (and therefore the food source).

It is easy to lament the passing of a golden era, but regretful and sad as some of these changes are, all cultures are constantly changing. Anyone would encourage disarmament, and hopefully it will occur, but towns are now an irreversible part of northern Kenya. Many of the developments in the towns are positive – no one enjoys walking twelve hours to fetch water, no one enjoys being ill and not having access to basic medication, and every child has a right to have their mind stimulated and their potential tapped by attending school. But it does mean that those living away from the majority of their cattle (in towns) are more vulnerable in times of drought.

Livestock are everything to families living in such an environment, even those in the towns. They are utterly dependent on their animals, their aim always is to preserve them and ensure they grow in number. If a drought comes their thinking is not 'We ought to eat these animals now because tomorrow they might be dead'; it is more 'we must not eat these animals now because they may survive and be our only hope for the future'. During the sustained drought leading up to 2000, many animals died. Had their shepherds known which ones were going to die, had they known the drought would last so long, they would have managed their flocks to last longer and provide more food. The trouble is they always hope the rain cloud will arrive on tomorrow's wind, and if only they could get their cattle through until that downpour, grass would soon appear and they would survive and multiply into the future.

As it was that rain cloud rarely appeared and so their life security suffered; with the dead animals went the vital source of food. Inevitably the drought had terrible consequences on the nutritional status of the population. It is generally agreed that if 10 per cent of the children are acutely malnourished then that is an emergency. In northern Kenya it was well over 40 per cent – a tragically high percentage which warranted a feeding response. When I arrived in 2001 another six months of feeding was required before an exit, so we set up feeding centres for malnourished children covering an area the size of East Anglia. The process of curing a child from malnutrition is a long one which involves regular feeding, monitoring of weight and checking for illness. This was supported by trying to educate the mothers in feeding practices, hygiene practices, best weaning habits and prevention of disease and by training local Ministry of Health staff in treating malnutrition for future droughts.

In Korr I used to play football in the local team. As I sat there during one half-time team talk, I noticed that my skinny legs were easily the largest set there. Most of my team-mates were aged between sixteen and twenty-two. Almost all of them lived through or were born around the time of the 1984 famine. These guys were the survivors. Being malnourished early on in your life has lasting effects on your physique (and sometimes IQ) and my team-mates were living evidence of this. Everyone in the area had been affected by drought in some way or at one time or another.

During my six months, there was one question I discussed in a variety of forms with local leaders, doctors, missionaries of twenty years, the mothers in our programme, PhD academics in Marsabit, development experts and highly paid consultants. The question was how to prevent this same terrible situation occurring in the next drought. There have always been droughts and there will undoubtedly be more. Much evidence, both scientific and anecdotal, points to droughts becoming more regular now than ever before, but what needs to be put in place between now and the next one? If our aim is to give a man a rod, what does that rod look like in this context? Restocking, income generation, changing livelihoods will all help but these are a people that are extremely vulnerable. Forty years ago, droughts were less common; now the population has grown and droughts increase in frequency and there is no easy solution.

Compared to Sudan and Burundi, those in northern Kenya had better access to education (though it was still poor), but both Sudan and Burundi have fertile soil which supports crops. With Sudan and Burundi it is easier to see how in the absence of a war people could subsist and survive, but in northern Kenya there had been no war. Of all the places I have worked in, northern Kenya seems the toughest environment to maintain a livelihood. It is the place where I have repeatedly and mostly deeply been struck by the absolute poverty.

Newsletter Home

Shortly into my assignment in Kenya I wrote the following in a letter:

> Part of our education work is focusing on HIV and AIDS prevention. Knowledge and understanding about the disease is still very limited. The disease is a potential time bomb in some areas of northern Kenya. With a very 'open' culture and almost every woman circumcised[1], it is conceivable that in fifteen years' time villages will be decimated by the virus as has happened elsewhere. 'My people are destroyed from lack of knowledge.'[2]

A married man left Korr for Nairobi to earn some money. He worked as a watchman and after many years he returned to his wife. He stayed four days before leaving again and soon was found dead from Aids. His wife, who had remained faithful, then tested positive. How tragic that what God intended as the most beautiful and intimate act of love results in death.

At times when I look at the long term picture for these people – permanently on the edge of existence, the population rising, the climate changing, the desert expanding...and then I think of similar situations in Sudan and Burundi, only with chronic war added to the equation – I wonder why. We don't have the answers, no one does. Even the greatest theologian (Paul) admitted to being 'perplexed'.

Somehow, we trust that God can use our mouldy loaves and rotten fishes. Why he chooses to work through humans, muppets as we are, I do not understand. But as I spend a day in the hot sun weighing Rendille children, I see in them and their mothers human characteristics common to us all: confidence, charm, beauty, intelligence, timidity, humour, cheek; a crying baby here, a chattering mother there. Suddenly these people are no longer beaded nomads I cannot relate to. They are my brother, my sister, my mother, my friend; alike in every way. Each of them is loved by God, and for moments I catch a tiny glimpse of that love.

For some reason God ordained them, and not me, to be born into a desert, where from day one they are destined to be starved. Starved of water, starved of food, starved of books, prams, Action Men, footballs, TVs, mobiles, shops, education…again, though I have been a Christian long enough to know why there is suffering in this world, I can't supply the answer. I understand the explanations, but struggle with the reasons.

So, perplexed? Certainly. Hard pressed on all sides? Yes. Struck down? Occasionally. Persecuted? Maybe. But crushed? In despair? Destroyed? Abandoned? No! 'For we [as Christians], fix our eyes not on what is seen, but on what is unseen. For what is seen is temporary, but what is unseen is eternal.'[3] And that is what gives us the hope, courage and strength to persevere.

Mother and Child

Evidently his visit was urgent. It was about 7.00 p.m., already dark, and we were just driving through the gate to our base. We had left at 6.00 a.m. that morning and, after meetings in Marsabit and then with some chiefs in a village, were feeling tired. As we entered the gate we saw the head chief of Korr. Usually this meant a polite thirty-minute conversation over a cup of tea before we got to the point of the visit.

This time he was there on behalf of a pregnant mother. This woman had been in labour about thirty-six hours ago, but something went wrong. During labour the arm had come out, but the head, body and legs remained inside her and died. She remained in her manyatta for about twelve hours and then decided to walk the 13 kilometres into Korr. The clinic had turned her away and now she was lying in a lot of pain in a hut opposite our camp.

Stephen, the Tearfund nurse, went and assessed the situation. A 'prolapsed' arm was the diagnosis. Apparently one had to push the arm back in, turn the child and then out the deceased baby should come. A relatively simple procedure, the trouble was there was a very high danger of tearing the uterus. Once that happens, she would bleed to death unless operated on immediately. I had seen a woman bleed to death before so realised the gravity of the situation. (I have subsequently heard of a similar case in Sudan where the local traditional healer arrived at the scene, cut off the head and each limb of the child whilst she was inside the woman and removed the child segment by segment. Thankfully that wasn't practiced here.)

We had to get to Marsabit where there were both doctors and operating rooms capable of dealing with the problem. The clinic had a vehicle but refused to take her. It was in the middle of the rainy season so parts of the road had turned into a lake and were therefore unpassable. The only route now was to follow car tracks through the desert which during daylight was a two-hour journey. At night it would take longer and be harder to follow. Once on the main road to Marsabit there was a further two hour drive through bandit country.

One would only consider such a journey in a life and death situation. Mega Dudu, the driver, and I took a quick shower, wolfed down some food, loaded the woman and her relatives onto a mattress and drove off into the night. Mega had the local knowledge and ten years' experience of driving in these conditions.

We had to stop to allow the mother to vomit. I could never imagine the pain and discomfort she was going through bouncing around in a pick-up. (I have given a number of lifts to people who have never before been in a vehicle – on a bumpy road the process of being bounced around a moving metal cage is completely alien to their senses – like a novice on the high seas they invariably become ill and throw up).

We kept a good pace and Mega navigated us to the main road, with one hyena sighted en route. From there it was two hours of the back-jarring 'corrugated-iron' road. We were both tired and I was struggling to stay awake. Thankfully Mega was made of sterner stuff and got us to the hospital, after midnight. It had taken more time than it would take to drive from London to Cornwall. We took the mother into the ward and awoke the duty nurse. We asked where the doctor was, and scurried off to break his slumber and drag him out of his cosy bed.

This woman was clearly and unquestionably tough. She had just gone through nine months of pregnancy, followed by the inevitable gruelling labour in forty-degree heat. After a day with a dead child inside her she had walked over 13 kilometres with the dead arm protruding between her legs; she had been rejected by the clinic, waited another six hours, been thrust into the back of a pick-up, bounced around for over four hours against its metal sides, and now was in hospital with someone prodding and pushing her dead child. They got the arm back inside her and thankfully the child came out smoothly without tearing the uterus.

I have spoken to a midwife about it since and she said that this is a relatively simple case to have dealt with during labour and could have been prevented. Any half-trained midwife in the UK would have spotted the problem and turned the child before the arm came out. This woman living in a set of huts in the middle of the desert did not have access to even the most basic midwifery care and as a result is without her beautiful God-given child.

Once we knew the mother was safe and in good hands, we went and slept. We got up the next morning, ate breakfast and went back to the hospital where the staff were ready to discharge her (we later found out they had not even prescribed any antibiotics). They needed something to transport the dead child. Someone was sent and duly fetched a makeshift coffin from the back of a store. It was an emptied cardboard box, the size of a shoe box, previously used for contraception storage. That was all that could be found for this life that never quite was. The little corpse was squeezed into the cardboard contraption – designed to transport condoms to prevent conception, it was now used to hide the failed result.

Soon we all set off for the journey home. Once off the

main road, about an hour's drive from the nearest settlement we heard a tap on the roof and were signalled to
stop. The two relatives got off the vehicle, bowed their
heads for a moment's silence, carried the box and placed
it reverently under a shrub not 10 yards away. They
prayed, returned slowly to the vehicle and signalled us to
proceed. We left the child for the hyenas – it would probably have been a matter of hours before they arrived. As
we drove on, my mind tried to calculate how many countless, nameless, lives – be they mothers or babies – were
needlessly lost in rural Africa every year. Thousands?
Hundreds of thousands? More than that?

On the return journey, I learnt the words to the following song by Graham Kendrick[4] which seemed to express
the gospel so well. Since then, every time I sing it, images
of that journey flash through my mind. Seldom are my
eyes still dry by the end.

From heav'n you came, helpless babe,
entered our world, your glory veiled;
not to be served but to serve,
and give your life that we might live.

This is our God, the Servant King,
he calls us now to follow him,
to bring our lives as a daily offering
of worship to the Servant King.

So let us learn how to serve,
and in our lives enthrone him;
each other's needs to prefer,
for it is Christ we're serving.

Nearly five years later, back in England, I was driving up the A3 only hours after the birth of my first child. Rachel and Iona were peacefully resting in hospital. Images of the miracle that is birth were swirling around in my mind and I marvelled in awe at the skill, commitment and abilities of the midwife who delivered our precious daughter. At the same time my memory cast back to that incident in Marsabit and I considered again how unfair it is that such care is not universally available.

Monastic Living

A few months into my time in northern Kenya, I came face to face with the shock recognition that I had been living a lifestyle similar to that of a monk. Whilst it was only for a matter of months, I could not escape the fact there were many parallels to a monastic livelihood: I was living in a community with about six other people (all of whom were Kenyans), we were all believers, we worked during the day and at night we fellowshipped. My life was a simple one: I was spending virtually no money, as there was so little to buy, and there were few comforts. We had no television, no newspapers, no running water and going to the loo involved walking 20 metres, downwind, to a seatless pit latrine. As a Christian organisation we did not drink as it might have offended the local Christians who linked alcohol with debauchery. Also similar to the monastic life was that I was celibate, with no girlfriend and no possible way of falling in love. (Whilst the women of the Rendille tribe are enormously beautiful, the cultural and linguistic gap between them and me was too great for me to contemplate a relationship.)

In Britain there are stimulants everywhere. You are never free from sights and sounds to fill and arouse your thinking. TV, radio, videos, music, adverts, billboards and newspapers seem almost omnipresent, hustling and bustling for attention. Undoubtedly these invade and affect your mind and attitudes. The first video I watched after weeks in Korr was a typical Hollywood film with the usual level of violence. Before watching it I had not seen any description of violence for weeks, and it was as though the surface of my mind had been cleansed of such images. Following the film it was awash with flashbacks; as involuntarily my brain brought to the forefront of my thoughts these scenes of fighting. I found myself pondering violent scenes, where just days previously I had not. Clearly the pictures, words and sounds, had affected my mind.

In northern Kenya (and other assignments) living a secluded lifestyle, I escaped many images one is unable to in the West, and in turn my mind and thoughts were freed and I could fill them with more healthy images. Every day, driving through the desert, I stared at the colours of the sun reflecting off the sand, wondered at the majesty of the mountains in the distance, enjoyed the striding ostrich, the occasional zebra and once or twice the breathtaking beauty of a giraffe. I read Christian books and learnt the words to famous old hymns. Never before or since had I such a sustained period of time without the bombardment of media, nor had I the chance to control what went into my mind and to try to fill it with wholesome thoughts.

Despite all this I was still left dealing daily with an

enormous power within me. What I realised more keenly in northern Kenya, was the strength of the sexual fire which lives within. Despite being almost completely unfuelled and without any 'provocation' by media images it remained a constant and powerful companion. The desires are inextricably linked with loneliness, a longing for companionship and intimacy and 'mateship', a need to be loved and to love, a need to be touched and to touch and much more. Our sexuality, it appears, is so well developed in us, it is such a dynamic and living instinct, that we cannot escape it. It is not dependent on outside stimuli; it exists and continues unabated. I realised more clearly in northern Kenya than ever before that celibacy is a huge burden because you cannot forget or avoid your desires. I decided it was a burden I was happy to carry until marriage, at the same time realising it was bearable only in the hope of marriage.

At times we Christians (myself included) appear so quick to condemn people for their sexual sins and ashamedly slow to empathise and understand. In light of Jesus' words 'woe to you, because you load people down with burdens they can hardly carry',[5] I sometimes feel Christians could further reflect on the burden of sexuality and be more sensitive and gracious as a result.

The Warrior God

Translated literally, in the Rendille language 'her' (pronounced 'there') means 'warrior', and this term applies to any circumcised young man not yet married in the Rendille tribe. The warriors roam the desert plains grazing their animals, charged with guarding the family's prized belongings. They are an incredible and striking people – tall, elegant, strong, well decorated with beaded arm bands and colourful headwear, red-haired and not usually wearing more than a loin cloth. These men are not short of milk, on which they survive. Despite a limited diet they cut impressive figures, not an inch of fat on them and built to walk, they are lean and fit, usually carrying a spear in one hand.

I found myself fascinated by these warriors. Once they had graduated from the home, their role, for up to fourteen years, was to go out and tend the livestock, often with just one or two other males and maybe – if they were lucky – an unmarried female for company. It was their task to, if necessary, fend off other tribes and regularly they had to deal with wild animals attacking their herd. Rendille folklore is full of stories of brave 'her' wrestling with lions and hyenas. Their morning began by milking the animals and they were extremely close to them. In lambing season it was not uncommon to see these strong young men striding with spear in one hand and lamb in the other. Regularly these stalwart warriors, able and trained to defend and fight, would bend down to sensitively care for the weakest lambs and sing songs of praise to their prize camel, bull, or goat.[6]

The warriors knew and could read the land brilliantly – searching always for pastures new. Then twice a year if the rains were good and grass was available near their homes they would take the long journey back and there be welcomed by friends, family and clan. A hero's return awaited them which they no doubt embellished with many stories of adventure and excitement. In our final few weeks at Korr the rains came. I think it rained twice: only two heavy downpours, but that was enough. Grass seeds that had laid dormant for months or even years sprouted and covered the yellow-brown sand with a light green. God tinted the landscape with his seasonal paintbrush and not long after the animal and human population swelled with new livestock and men. The atmosphere changed to one far more festive, cheerful and confident as these 'her' bestrode the town.

I was a similar age to these men, and for some reason it felt the right way for men of our age to be; travelling nomadically through the open country, trained for exploration. In a strange way I found myself envying them – harking for an age past when men were bred for such activities. The same side of men which draws them to the armed forces (quest for adventure, heroics) is in me, and was touched by their lifestyle. I not only admired them but also could in a strange way relate to them. Subconsciously I found myself drawing comfort from their lifestyle as there seemed to be a strange symmetry between theirs and mine.

I too spent many months a long way from family, some of it involved adventure, much of it felt very lonely. I could imagine how they, like me, must have longed to be at home, must have waited eagerly for the rains and I could imagine their sense of excitement on the long return journey. In those final weeks I too was on my home journey – it was a winding road of closing the feeding sites, saying the goodbyes, driving down to Nairobi, and flying back to the UK. I had been away for sixteen months[7] and my everything was geared to returning. On return, the warriors would spend the night dancing under the stars with the local girls who dressed especially for the occasion. I arrived back a couple of days before Christmas and landed right in the middle of party season and reunions – on Christmas Eve we went to the pub, filled with old school friends most of whom I had not seen for many years. Family occasions, New Year's Eve parties, and curries with mates exchanging stories all greeted me on my return.

I also learnt from the 'her' what it meant to be a shepherd. Shepherds lead from the back. They point their animals in the right direction and follow. The animals are guided by steady but faint corrections from behind – usually a whistle or a call, often a few gentle taps on the side of a sheep straying from the path. From behind they could see everything; all they needed to know was in front of them: their animals, the path, the mountains, the sun and skies. Only occasionally would any real vigour be needed and that usually was the result of a calamitous event such a vehicle tearing past, scaring the animals and causing them to run off. Then the shepherds would run after them and steer them back in the right direction.

So I admired them, could relate to them, learnt from them and also better understood God from observing them. Does not God lead from behind as well? At times perhaps God lets us walk ahead whilst all the time watching us carefully. Are not his instructions gentle and regular? 'Whether you turn to the right or the left, your ears will hear a voice behind you, saying, "This is the way; walk in it"'.[8] These strong, all-powerful men of the community were fit to fight and ready to defend their people against outside threats and opposing tribes. The land was theirs, they bestrode it powerfully and confidently, they knew every mountain, every type of tree. They might have 100 goats but all were known by name. And yet there they were, evidently full of love for each one – happy to pick up the frailest lamb in their arms and carry it along the journey. So strong in one breath and yet able to bend down, to clean, caress and care for the tiniest infant lamb in the other; able to hold it close to their chest, to feed it, to bathe it, to be its father and its mother. So too God 'gathers the lambs in his arms and carries them close to his heart'.[9] On the long and lonely evenings it was this verse that I drew on the most. Enfolded in God's powerful arms, I, a tender lamb, held by such strength and yet such tender love all at once.

Notes

1. Circumcised women are likely to bleed more during intercourse and therefore the infection rate increases.
2. Hosea 4:6.
3. 2 Corinthians 4:18.
4. Extract taken from the song *The Servant King* by Graham Kendrick copyright © 1983 Thankyou Music.
5. Luke 11:46.
6. In another part of northern Kenya I was sitting in a meeting and a child near me was playing with a goat by caressing and yanking his hairy testicles – as no one else seemed to bat an eyelid I found myself assuming this, culturally, was a perfectly normal way to show affection to a young goat.
7. I had been back to England a couple of times on holiday.
8. Isaiah 30:21.
9. Isaiah 40:11.

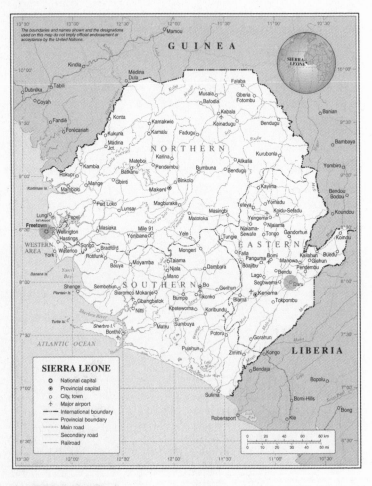

Population	6,005,250 (estimate 2006)	Religion	60% Muslim, 10% Christian, 30% indigenous
Population Growth	2.3%	Language	English
Prevalence of HIV	7%	Literacy	29%
People Living with HIV/AIDS	170,000	Life Expectancy	40

CHAPTER FIVE

From Northern Kenya to Sierra Leone

Leaving Northern Kenya was sad but also exciting. Goodbyes are often easier for those leaving than those left behind. I was upset to say goodbye, but looking forward to going home. My last day in Kenya was spent in a game reserve enjoying a final African sunset. That night I boarded a plane and early the next morning landed in Heathrow. I sat on the bus home and watched the same sun I saw set sixteen hours before in Kenya rise over the English countryside. It was crisp and frosty, the first winter's day I had seen in nearly three years.

It is said that on coming home you can find feelings of anger, hurt, resentment and confusion. Whilst on one level I loved being home, on another I think I felt all of those emotions. Tearfund sends everyone for a psychological medical on their return and to my surprise I spent most of that hour in tears. I do not really know why, though I really appreciated the fact that for one hour, someone was prepared to do nothing but listen to me.

In part those tears reflected the feeling that the three countries I had worked in appeared such desperate cases. As much as I stared at them, I found it hard to find too much hope. Burundi seemed to be getting nowhere in their peace process, Sudan even less so, and my friends in northern Kenya would always remain vulnerable to drought – in four years' time another would come with the same crippling results.[1]

I was soon thinking about another assignment. I had been in Burundi when thousands had been forced into camps and yet there was virtually no money around to support them. Meanwhile in the Balkans, millions was being spent for what appeared a lower level of need. Aid is not always evenly distributed and a part of me was keen not to follow the latest 'headline disaster' (at that time Afghanistan); supporting a country in need but out of the spotlight appealed. So when Sierra Leone came on the horizon it interested me. One of the reasons for this was that it felt like a country with hope.

Sierra Leone

Sierra Leone was repeatedly ranked as the poorest country in the world in many of the UN reports of the late 1990s and early 2000s yet with the natural resources at its disposal, it could, however, have a very high GDP.

The capital, Freetown, (so named by William Wilberforce as a home for freed slaves) is positioned in the tropics of West Africa. With humidity usually over 95 per cent, the land is fertile, so the markets are rich with a huge variety of fruit and vegetables, their range of bright colours matched by the dazzling headscarves and African dresses worn by the women at the stalls. The land has been 'blessed' with diamonds and other minerals, and the white sandy beaches are as romantic as any in the world – perfect for tourism. Before the war there was a reasonable road infrastructure together with schools and hospitals. It contained all the ingredients for a successful economy and prosperous nation.

But high unemployment in the 1980s, coupled with incompetent and corrupt officials fuelled disillusionment with the Government. The Revolutionary United Front (RUF), led in part by Foday Sankoh, began to take root. In neighbouring Liberia, a civil war was being waged and the rebels in Sierra Leone were able to receive consignments of weapons and other support from over the border as well as from Colonel Gaddafi in Libya. The porous borders meant it was easy to attack and disappear into the jungles of Liberia. Soon however the RUF gained strongholds in the south-east of the country, which contained the majority of the nation's diamonds. Inevitably the most devastated areas were those around the diamond mines. Throughout the 1990s Liberia was exporting more diamonds than any other country in the region and yet it does not own a single diamond mine. They were robbed from rebel-held land in Sierra Leone. At its height it is estimated the RUF diamond trade amounted to US$100 million per year.[2] The main importers were Western countries, with the Netherlands topping the list. Our love of the inanimate largely useless object has fuelled the deaths of 1000s of treasured people.

As the war grew it became more barbaric and bloody, 'unrivalled in all of Africa in terms of senseless horror and brutality'.[3] Towns were devastated while village upon village was completely and utterly flattened. Cement foundations were all that remained of homes, churches, schools, 'barazas' (public buildings), hinting at what the town or village once was. The number of dead was estimated at 100,000, not as many as Rwanda, but the weaponry used in Sierra Leone was far heavier and consequentially the physical destruction greater. In Kailahun district alone, over 100 primary schools were destroyed. Once again a generation of children grew up without an education.

I visited two former hospitals, one in Kailahun and one in Swegwema. Together they stand as the most chilling buildings I have ever been into. The buildings of Swegwema hospital, most of which remained standing, pointed to a highly sophisticated pre-war hospital. Now however, it was soulless; haunted by a ghostly emptiness. Before the war it had everything, long wards for hundreds of beds, laboratories, rest rooms, waiting rooms, maternity units, houses for nurses, training schools for nurses, homes for doctors, top class water pumps near every door, a small chapel and much more. Built by the Methodists, it was large and neatly laid out over acres of land. Now, however, it was utterly vacant: the beds were strewn in every direction, the windows smashed, broken tiles were all that remained on the roofs, plaster was chipping off walls now splattered by bullet holes, the water pumps no longer worked. The rebels had ransacked it, emptied it and used it as their base. Pictures that had hung on the walls were now replaced by graffiti etchings of machine-guns, rocket-propelled grenade launchers and tanks accompanied by RUF slogans. There were a few reminders of the hospital as it once was: on one wall there was a sign reading 'in-patients', on another, 'cashier', but mostly the only signs left were ones of abuse and dereliction. I visited the hospital three times. It was only on my third visit I realised why it felt so eerie: it was completely devoid of any other person; there were no children following us. In Africa, children are always with you, certainly in a densely populated country like Sierra Leone. If you step out of your house some little kid will be waving at you and calling after you; if you go for a walk you are followed by a gaggle of kids. Like the pied piper, where ever you go you can be certain to be followed; except, that is, when you enter the deserted Swegwema hospital.

The RUF, bereft of political aims or objectives, were driven by lust for power and savagery. Earning the title of 'African Khmer Rouge' their rebel units were given spine-chilling names like 'Cut Hands Commando.' Another unit was called 'Kill Man No Blood' whose speciality was beating people to death without a drop of blood being spilt. In other places torture included writing on pieces of paper sentences such as: 'cut off limbs', 'cut off genitals', 'slice off lips', and then force their victims to pick one and read it out – thereby pronouncing their next punishment. Mass rapes and sexual mutilations were designed to destroy the very essence of the victim's humanity. Fathers were forced to watch their sons being buggered and their daughters gang-raped. Pregnant women would have their belly sliced open and their unborn child yanked out as rebels took bets on the gender of the baby.

Sierra Leone, epitomised perhaps more than any other country, the use of children in war. This is not a new tactic; countries have been using children for as long as there have been soldiers. But the practice of using them in Sierra Leone seems to have shocked more than most. Children as young as six years old were recruited into the rebel armies. One renowned and feared commander, looking after a troop of soldiers in Freetown, was only eight.

Children were often used as the first wave of attack in the battles. They would be given hallucinatory drugs, often powdered into gashes in their temple. These drugs would give them a crazed bravery with which they would charge an enemy line, dodging around with ecstasy-like energy, firing away with their Kalashnikov. Children, not yet teenagers, were regular killers and comfortable with their art. They had been forced into it the first time, then it became a habit and finally almost an addiction. The gun gave them an enormous power. Now old men were forced to obey orders from someone whose voice had not yet broken. Women were forced to lie down, as young teenagers exercised every sick benefit that power would bring.

The other gross characteristic of this war was amputations. Part of the rebel tactics in casting psychological fear into the minds of the population was to cut limbs off. It seemed no one, no matter how vulnerable, was off limits. I heard of a six-month-old child whose hand was chopped at the wrist. Freetown (the capital) is pocketed with camps for amputees, where experts from all over the world try to support limbless patients.

And so the war continued, mostly unnoticed by the West. In 1998 the Nigerians nobly sent in their troops to try to sort out the problems. But they were unable to turn the tide as Freetown came under wave after wave of heavily armoured attack. Eventually the UN sent in a peacekeeping force in 1999. Over 100 UN forces were captured by the RUF in the south-east of the country. As it became obvious the peacekeepers were struggling, the British deployed forces in 2000. They secured the airport and crucial areas of Freetown. Initially sent in to evacuate British citizens, the British troops remained and were a crucial force which helped turn the tide in the battle for Sierra Leone. From there the rebels were always on the losing side and the peacekeeping forces, now up to 16,000 (the largest peacekeeping forces in the world ever), were able to stabilise the country.

Ahmed Tejan Kabbah was the president, and had spent more than twenty years working in the UN system. In the early 1990s he joined the politics of his country and spent a lot of the 1990s on the run and in refuge. He was popular with the people and led the way in urging people to forgive the rebels and move on. Backing his tough words with actions, he made Foday Sankoh (leader of the RUF) his deputy in 1999. This was a dangerous political gamble, but one which revealed the true character of both men. Foday soon opened fire into a crowd in Freetown, killing twenty people, which was enough to put him in jail and bring him to justice. In the end he died in jail.

To see leaders who pillaged the country and were responsible for killing and maiming thousands behind bars and undergoing trials is of huge psychological benefit for a country. In the years following the war a number of key rebel leaders were captured and brought to trial while others were killed or died. Forgiveness is a vital ingredient, but it is only part of the recipe; justice and forgiveness together do a much better job of healing a nation.

Elections in May 2002 confirmed Kabbah as the people's choice and everyone could get on with the huge and difficult task of rebuilding the country. I arrived just before the election and it was a privilege to be a tiny part of the rebuilding process. I worked with people who had suffered years of misery, now joyful in their hope for their country. Tearfund was working in the south-east of the country, not far from the diamond mines, in villages which had been completely destroyed. The aim was to help refugees resettle and rebuild their lives.

The returning population, most of whom had been living in refugee camps in neighbouring Liberia or Guinea, were only able to drink from the muddy swamps as almost every well had been destroyed. Tearfund provided water and sanitation. Being part of a project that dug wells, capped springs and provided sanitation facilities was enormously gratifying. Unlike feeding a child, where the impact was vital but short-term, wells would supply hundreds of people with clean water for years to come. Sierra Leone recorded some of the highest infant mortality rates in the world; most of the children died from preventable diseases such as diarrhoea. Our water and sanitation work coupled with our health education saw a dramatic decline in diarrhoea and other water-borne diseases in the villages where we worked, proving our work was vital to health. We also worked with the Tearfund partner on peace-building and reconciliation projects.

Are You The One?

Daru, where I lived, felt like a town in celebration. At least three nights a week a disco was thrown as the people partied into the early hours. The Sierra Leonians seemed to have an exuberant, buoyant, unreserved nature – readily able to laugh and dance. Our accommodation was in the heart of the town and so sleep was often mixed with the sound of loud thumping music followed, a little later, by the Muslim call to prayer.

I was struck by the high rate of sickness and mortality among our staff compared to other countries in which I had worked. This was partly a reflection of the poor sanitation and health facilities and partly a reflection of the fact that we were in the tropics where diseases spread faster. In my diary I wrote:

I was just thinking about the number of our staff who have had close relatives die in the three months I have been here. Just last weekend Ibrahim Nyalley lost his wife in childbirth. The child died too. He is left bringing up a beautiful little girl (his first daughter) without a mother. Eric's wife lost her brother, Amara lost his father. That is four in a weekend!

I doubt whether I could bring to mind everyone else we have prayed for who has lost a relative since I have been here. Sheku lost a close relative and broke down in tears in one prayer time. Another lost his newly born child, and then his wife, and then his mother in the space of a few months [a few months after I left he also died, probably from Aids]. And we only have around thirty staff here. If I think of all the people I know back in the UK it is probably more than 100, most of whom I have known for many years. Of those I can think of only two that have lost a close relative. Compare that to just a few months here.

Our staff ranged from devout Muslim, to nominal Muslim, to nominal Christian to devout Christian. Every morning we gathered to read through Luke's Gospel and discuss the meaning of the passages. It provided some fascinating discussions and insights as everyone spoke from their different perspectives. In the context of Sierra Leone, Jesus' words 'Love your enemies, do good to those who hate you, bless those who curse you, pray for those who mistreat you'[4] carried huge resonance. Discussing them with colleagues who had seen friends burn their houses and kill their relatives was a humbling experience, the more so as many came round to agree with the words of Jesus.

It was my first experience of working with, and in, a strongly Muslim area and it forced me to consider where Mohammed belonged in relation to Jesus. Why should I believe in Jesus' words rather than Mohammed's? What made Christianity the 'right' religion? Born into a Muslim setting, with loving parents, would I not also be a Muslim? In those morning devotions I discovered John the Baptist asked Jesus a similar question: 'Are you the one who was to come, or should we expect someone else?'[5] I had never understood Jesus' reply until I was in Sierra Leone. 'Go back and report to John what you have seen and heard: The blind receive sight, the lame walk, those who have leprosy are cured, the deaf hear, the dead are raised and the good news is preached to the poor.'[6] Should I believe in Jesus or Mohammed? Was Jesus as he claimed he was – the Son of God – or was he, as Mohammed claimed, a prophet? Why should I believe Jesus' statement above Mohammed'? Jesus' reply helped me see that uniquely he backed his own claims about himself with a spiritual authority – he healed the sick, he gave people sight, he performed miracles. Mohammed didn't. Mohammed was an incredible leader and is an inspiration for millions. However, for me, Jesus' life showed evidence of a divinity which assures my sometimes wobbly faith: he raised people from the dead and lived a life of peace. Mohammed was involved in wars and was polygamous; Jesus abstained and liberated women through his words, miracles and actions. Where Mohammed was buried, he remained; where Jesus was laid in the tomb he (unique to any man who ever lived) came back to life and never died thereafter. His life gives his words authority.

Reflections on Loneliness

Whilst I loved my time in Sierra Leone, I was once again alone 'in the bush', miles from family and friends, and I began thinking and reading about loneliness.

Following the 2002 Bam earthquake in Iran which killed over 10,000 people and destroyed an entire town, the *Guardian Weekly* interviewed a woman who had lost over forty members of her family. She had been out of the town for a shopping trip at the time of the earthquake and came back to find that everyone she knew and loved was dead. She described loneliness as 'having no one to share your grief with'. She would have known. On a smaller scale, loneliness can also be having no one to share your joy with. It can be having no one to share your thoughts with, no one to have a beer with. Those who have experienced solitary confinement say that, left only to your own thoughts and worries without any form of company, it is the worst of tortures.[7]

Loneliness has many forms and many symptoms. Cultural isolation is one. In Southern Sudan, I was the only white face in the town for the majority of my time there. The same was true in Korr, except for a missionary couple about thirty years older than me, and in Sierra Leone there was one other Western expat in the team and town. While I would not swap a single day of any assignment and treasure enormously the cross-cultural friendships which I made and maintain, there was an unavoidable cultural gap which fed the separation.

As well as cultural isolation the most obvious driver for loneliness was missing home, family and friends. Nelson Mandela writes:

> My commitment to my people, to the millions of South Africans I would never know or meet, was at the expense of the people I knew best and loved most.[8]

A few years in the bush is nothing compared with the colossal sacrifices of Nelson Mandela, but in a very tiny way, I could relate to his words. I was giving all my energies to unknown faces, people whose language I could not speak, people whose culture I did not share nor ever would share. I missed my family and friends enormously. I recall happily giving piggy backs to a whole bunch of young children – and seeing the joy it gave them and then suddenly remembered, with a pang, the times I had refused my sister similar piggy backs. I felt a wave of guilt for giving all these children, whose names I didn't know, whose faces I cannot now recall, love and attention I had refused my sister many times.

In Sierra Leone, I learnt to trust that relationships can grow even while apart, and drew a lot from reading Henri Nouwen's book *Reaching Out: The Three Movements of Spiritual Life*. He encourages us to see solitude as a positive and helps explain how. Three quotations were particularly helpful:

> In our solution-orientated world it is more important than ever to realize that wanting to alleviate pain without sharing it is like wanting to save a child from a burning house without the risk of being hurt.
>
> (Henri Nouwen)

> When you part from your friend, you grieve not; for that which you love most in him may be clearer in his absence, as the mountain to the climber is clearer from the plain. (Kahil Gibran)

> It is in deep solitude that I find the gentleness with which I can truly love my brothers. (Thomas Merton)

There are more subtle ways loneliness affects one too. Often the very nature of the landscape and environment adds to the solitude. Both the thick jungle in Sierra Leone, which diligently engulfs and powerfully pervades everything around it, and the breadth of the desert in northern Kenya – so vast, wide and utterly infertile – can make you feel insignificant and small. In a similar way the lack of hills in Sudan also added to the isolation. There is neither anything to look up to nor anything from which you can gain a different perspective; there isn't a 'view'. The place is all bush, so rarely could you see more than 200 yards. At night the sky is massive – surrounding you, entrapping you, reminding you of your tininess.

In the West we have created a world which blocks out this vast expanse of emptiness called the sky. We have built buildings, we live in homes. On the walls we put pictures, often of ourselves. We listen to radios or watch TV which fulfils our need for companionship. Everything is designed to make our life easier and to serve us: remote controls, cookers, TV and the internet are all under our control and therefore our subconscious will logically make us think that we, with all these objects serving us, are important.

In Sudan, if I wanted water I had to walk about 200 yards, pump very hard for about five minutes before water, from 40 metres below the ground, had filled a 20 litre jerrycan – which in turn had to be transported back to my house, boiled and filtered before use. In Britain if you want water you turn a tap. A tap is there to serve you and provides you with a beautiful, unlimited supply of water. It makes you feel good. In Sudan getting water makes you feel enslaved to the earth. Subtle as these things are; they probably affect one's psyche.[9] Being close to nature, dwarfed in comparison, adds to your feeling of 'aloneness'.

In addition to the environment around you, a lack of physical touch can add to loneliness. At one stage I probably went thirteen weeks without a hug. I shook hands plenty of times – but a decent, genuine, heartfelt embrace had not happened. The fact I can still remember the hug Fergus, my Programme Director, greeted me with on arrival in Nairobi, probably underlines how much I had unknowingly missed it. With hindsight I see a lack of physical touch was a subtle but significant cause of loneliness and subsequent lowness. I think it affected my psyche, moods and temperament. Nelson Mandela describes the first visit he was granted in Robben Island where he was not separated from the visitor by walls and glass:

> When Zeni [his daughter] saw me, she practically threw her tiny daughter to her husband and ran across the room to embrace me. I had not held my now-grown daughter virtually since she was about her own daughter's age. It was a dizzying experience...to suddenly hug one's fully grown child. I then embraced my new son and he handed me my tiny granddaughter whom I did not let go of for the entire visit. To hold a baby, so vulnerable and soft in my rough hands, hands that for too long had held only picks and shovels, was a profound joy. I don't think a man was ever happier to hold a baby than I was that day.

An orphanage, despite adequate medical and feeding care, found that many of their babies died. Investigations concluded that the cause of many deaths was that children were not being held and cuddled enough. Another experiment contrasted babies who were breastfed and cuddled by their parents with others that were held in an incubator and only touched at feeding time. After six weeks, despite the same quantity of milk being given to every child, those in the incubator had not grown beyond their birth weight whilst the rest were all above average.

We all need to be held and touched. To go without will affect us negatively. Maybe the woman in Iran could equally have said 'loneliness is not having anyone to hold you when you cry'.

I am sure in every society there must be those who need our physical touch. In New Testament times it was lepers. Herded and ostracised into a colony to prevent contamination, many were forced to wear a bell so others would keep their distance as they approached. When Jesus met the leper, before he said a word, he 'reached out his hand and touched the man'.[10] The leper had probably gone years without being touched. So for a man with Jesus' reputation to lovingly place his hand on his rotting body would have been almost as powerful as the healing itself; maybe it was a part of the healing. Perhaps Jesus understood this fundamental need to be touched and wants to reach us in our loneliness also.

Newsletter Home

This newsletter, sent during my six months in Sierra Leone, sums up my experience.

'Does God have authority to forgive a man who amputated the arm of a two-month-old child?' 'Should I forgive the person who attacked a heavily pregnant lady – killing the unborn child first?' 'Does loving your enemy mean welcoming your brother who fought and killed for the rebels?' 'Does God expect us to feed those that burnt down our houses?' Is this what the gospel means?

These are questions Christians face in Sierra Leone. It is a country going through an incredible phase. A ten-year civil war has ended, elections have passed smoothly and fairly, everyone seems happy with the outcome and therefore the whole nation appears to be dancing and enjoying themselves.

Yet still the reminders of the bitter fighting are all

around. I have never seen such destruction before: in certain districts every town, every village, every building has been laid waste. Hospitals, as large as any I have ever seen in rural Africa, are in utter disuse with all the buildings destroyed and no one there. As you wander round the empty wards covered in graffiti you read the slogans of former rebels who lived there only a few months past.

So the wounds must run deep: MSF[11] stated that 70 per cent of the population are clinically traumatised, one in four children die under the age of five and 50 per cent of the women who have been in contact with rebels have been raped. Scenes people have described to me seem the most articulate description of living hell I have ever heard.

And yet peace is here, and people living in one of the poorest countries in the world seem to be smiling. Tearfund is a part of the rebuilding process, although, as always, the need outweighs the supply and, honour as it is to be working here, it feels like a tiny drop in a vast ocean of need. In the district where we are working, bordering both Liberia and Guinea, over 30,000 people have returned from camps in the past two months. Many more are expected and they are returning to empty villages. Tearfund are providing water (over twenty wells) and over 500 latrines along with health education in some of these villages to help facilitate this resettlement. An old lady collecting her first bucket of clean water was unable to contain her joy and danced around the newly installed pump.

Religion here is a hotchpotch mix. A labourer fell down a well 'because he was pushed by a demon' and needed to sacrifice a few hens in atonement (I tried to point out there had been one all-encompassing, all-powerful sacrifice). Almost all belong to a 'secret society' that practices traditional 'bush craft' and ancestral beliefs. When someone falls ill they go to the clinic, and then visit a 'traditional' doctor. And yet most will claim allegiance to either Jesus or Allah if it suits or fits. My dreams are pierced every morning by the Muslim call to prayer.

Each morning we are studying the book of Luke with the staff. When reading Luke 5 (the healing of the paralytic) the questions of forgiveness were raised. It is in trying to answer these incredibly difficult and deep questions that one realises anew the power of the gospel.

'But where sin increased, grace increased all the more' (Romans 5:20). And so can it be with this country? Sin increased to kill tens of thousands. Now thousands of former soldiers are living in the same villages they once fought and killed over. Can it be that grace will increase all the more?

Please pray for this country and neighbouring Liberia which seems to be descending into war just as fast as Sierra Leone is coming out.

All love,
Ed

Notes

1. As it turned out that is exactly what happened. In 2006 Tearfund were forced to run another feeding programme in exactly the same locations.

2. Figure quoted by Damien Lewis in his book *Operation Certain Death*, Arrow, 2005.
3. Damien Lewis, *Operation Certain Death*, Arrow, 2005.
4. Luke 6:27.
5. Luke 7:20.
6. Luke 7:22.
7. Both Nelson Mandela and Martin Luther King speak of how hard they found the experience. The former wrote: 'I found solitary confinement the most forbidding aspect of prison life. There is no end and no beginning; there is only one's mind, which can begin to play tricks. Was that a dream or did it really happen? One begins to question everything. Did I make the right decision, was my sacrifice worth it? In solitary there is no distraction from these haunting questions.'
8. Nelson Mandela, *A Long Walk to Freedom*, Abacus, 1995.
9. Equally, I am sure that living in an urban jungle, alone in a block of flats, could do the same.
10. Matthew 8:3.
11. Médecins Sans Frontières (Doctors Without Borders), a medical aid agency.

Chapter Six

From Sierra Leone to Southern Sudan the Second Time

It was during my time in Sierra Leone that I realised I was in love with Rachel.

Rachel and I had first met on the Kenyan coast eighteen months before whilst on a break from northern Kenya and southern Sudan respectively. Shortly after first meeting, I remember staring at her feet thinking 'I don't believe it, I even find her feet attractive!' If I felt that way about her feet, imagine how I felt about the rest of her. So with lust at first sight assured, the love (and then finally commitment) followed. A nurse by background, she too has spent much of the past eight years overseas in relief work, in southern Sudan, Kosovo, northern Kenya, Afghanistan and the Democratic Republic of Congo. Our relationship was long distance until a few months before our wedding when, for the first time, we lived in the same country.

After six months in Sierra Leone I moved to a small town and relief centre called Lokichoggio in northern Kenya, which serves as the gateway to southern Sudan. Tearfund now had four bases in southern Sudan and I often visited them to try to offer support. By the time I left 18 months later, great strides were being made on the peace process, yet still it was hard to imagine the country, so undeveloped, with so few educated people, levering itself out of poverty.

A Tall and Smooth-Skinned People

If you wanted to make a case for southern Sudan being cursed it would not be difficult. The war in south Sudan ran for twenty years – the longest in Africa. Before that there were eleven years of peace which were preceded by another fifteen years of war. Before that they were colonised by the British. For decades before that the peoples were victims to raids from tribes stealing their children, running a slave trade that continues to this day.

Since independence, Sudan's Government has always been dominated by a small ethnic elite from central northern Sudan. The peripheral areas of the country complain of marginalisation and discrimination. While Sudan has experienced a number of violent conflicts since independence, the main civil war resumed in 1983. The war is fought mainly between the northern Government and southern tribes over a complex interaction of factors, including religion, wealth, power, oil and independence. While a small elite prosper, it has had a devastating effect on the country.

Driven by a lust for power and control of resources, the government has committed many atrocities and human rights abuses, even, some allege, ethnic cleansing and genocide. It has ordered the burning of villages by armed militia and used helicopter gunships and Antonovs to terrorise populations. Likewise the southern rebel armies have also received criticism over their human rights record. Intertribal conflicts, not least between the Nuer and Dinka, have been bloody and bitter and some say have accounted for more deaths than the fighting with the Government. In 2002 there were believed to be over twenty different rebel armies in the south. Many of the leaders of these armies are unelected and autocratic. They practiced forced conscription and recruited child soldiers, and were far from being accountable to their people.

The war crippled the country economically. Many places barely have a cash economy, preferring instead a bartering system; those places that do trade in cash have a confused mix of three currencies. Not many places in the world are as underdeveloped as south Sudan. The few remnants of development, such as schools and the odd brick building, had been almost completely flattened by 2004. Town after town was scarred by crumbling administrative buildings, constructed in the 1950s and 1970s (during the peace years), standing as derelict walls that shelter overgrown weeds and support neither roof nor windows. At least two generations grew up with virtually no education (in 2000 only 2 per cent of the population finished primary school). The only people I met in their twenties and thirties able to read and write had learnt as refugees, outside the country.

As I left, Sudan was on the brink of signing a peace deal but it was hard to see where she would find enough educated people to staff a civil service. Southern Sudan had extremely basic infrastructure with barely a slab of tarmac. For the twenty years preceding 2005, while the world moved on apace, southern Sudan has moved backwards. People who knew Rumbek in the 1960s and returned were shocked by how the place has declined.

Health care is vastly under-resourced. There have been

regular famines: 1988[1] and 1998 are the most recent and severe – each affecting hundreds of thousands of lives. Additionally in the late 1980s it is estimated that over 100,000 people died of the disease kala-azar.[2] It will be one of the last countries in the world to eradicate guinea worm (a parasite that lives in water and enters the human body breeding worms inside the human skin, sometimes in the most awkward of places). During the 18 months on this assignment there were many outbreaks of measles, an outbreak of yellow fever and whooping cough. At the same time as the outbreak of SARS made headline news after killing a few dozen, a whooping cough outbreak in southern Sudan killed over 200 people but barely made a few lines on an internet news site. Sudanese women have one of the highest death rates in childbirth of any country. Often they themselves are malnourished whilst pregnant, which some studies suggest will leave the child with a permanently low IQ. While in other countries, such as Malawi, donors will regularly fund a feeding programme if 5–8 per cent of the child population are acutely malnourished, in Sudan donors tend to support projects only when acute malnutrition is more than 15 per cent.

Such resources that they have seem to be out of the reach of southerners – massive oil reserves are controlled by the Government, who have systematically and brutally destroyed homes, burnt villages, killed cattle, and abducted children to drive nomadic populations off their ancestral land in an effort to reach the oil. People as poor and uneducated as any in the world, have for centuries been unknowingly grazing a land rich in oil reserves, and now, because of that wealth, have been driven from their land and forced into even greater poverty.

An estimated 2 million people have died in the war, over 4 million are thought to be refugees and 2 million internally displaced.

Perhaps as much as any country, hope for its future seemed bleak. People even say the Bible talks of Sudan as a land cursed:

> Woe to the land of whirring wings along the rivers of Cush... Go, swift messengers, to a people tall and smooth-skinned, to a people feared far and wide, an aggressive nation of strange speech, whose land is divided by rivers.
>
> For, before the harvest, when the blossom is gone and the flower becomes a ripening grape, he will cut off the shoots with pruning knives, and cut down and take away the spreading branches. They will be left to the mountain birds of prey and to the wild animals; the birds will feed on them all summer, and the wild animals all winter. (Isaiah 18:1–2, 5–6)

Some claim Genesis 2, when describing the Garden of Eden, watered by four rivers,[3] refers to Sudan. Southern Sudan is anything but paradise but it is easy enough to imagine that mankind might first have tasted evil, death and sin in such a place. Deadly snakes exist there and are widely believed to contain supernatural connections.

Although we know that the problems have been caused by man and not God, sometimes something deep inside feels that maybe Sudan is irredeemably blighted. Whilst working there I tried desperately to cultivate a heart and hope for Sudan and regularly pray for her, but staring at so many problems does blunt faith. In 2003 I wrote the following:

> Can God solve the longest running war in the world? Can God really convince the Government to give up oil revenues? Will they ever allow self-determination for the south which holds so many resources? Will people ever be held to account for their war crimes?

> 'Awake, Oh Lord! Why do you sleep? Rouse yourself! Do not reject us forever. Why do you hide your face and forget [their] misery and oppression? [They] are brought down to the dust; [their] bodies cling to the ground.'

> '[Facing] death all day long; [they] are considered as sheep to be slaughtered.'

> 'Rise up and help [them], redeem [them] because of your unfailing love.'   (Psalm 44:22–26)

> 'Will justice ever dwell in this desert?'
>   (Isaiah 32:16)

That is the nearest I can come to a genuine heartfelt prayer which goes beyond lip service. Yet history teaches us that the wheels of justice do roll on, that hope need not be conquered, that God, through co-workers of faith, does work tirelessly and that he keeps hearts from being overcome by despair. Certainly international pressure is bringing progress. Yet even with a peace process the road ahead seems terrifyingly long and treacherous.

Reading biographies of Bram Fischer in South Africa, Nelson Mandela, Ghandi and Martin Luther King revealed how giant men of faith can make headway and maintain a hope against seemingly hopeless odds. Martin Luther King wrote the following quotations whilst in the middle of a daunting struggle:

'During such moments our spirits are almost overcome by gloom and despair, and we feel that there is no light anywhere. But ever again we look toward the east and discover that there is another light which shines even in darkness and the "spear of frustration" is transformed "into a shaft of light".

'...the thing that makes me happy is that I can hear a voice crying through the Vista of time, saying "it may not come today or it may not come tomorrow, but it is well that it is within thine heart. It is well that you are trying". You may not see it. The dream may not be fulfilled, but it's just good that you have a desire to bring it into reality.'

'How Long? Not long, because no sin can live forever.
How long? Not long, because you still reap what you sow.
How Long? Not long, because the arm of the moral universe is long, but it bends toward justice.
How long? Not long because mine eyes have seen the glory of the coming of the Lord, His truth is marching on.
He has sounded forth the trumpets that shall never call retreat. He is lifting up the hearts of men before His

judgement seat. Oh be swift my soul to answer him. Be jubilant, my feet. Our God is marching on.'[4]

Searching harder, we can cling to glimmers of hope. There is massive potential in Sudan: strong people, living in a land rich for cattle with vast grazing areas, fertile land suitable for cultivation and agriculture. Each year God sends down huge reservoirs of water teeming with fish and water. There are large unused resources of the Nile waters and oil. The land has been blessed – maybe its richness can be tapped and prosperity can come. Strides forward have been made in southern Sudan, such progress was unimaginable even in 2001. Hopefully it will continue. Unjust regimes will always ultimately fail, as they seek to deny the most basic of God-given rights: that of freedom. People denied freedom will always rise up and eventually win for themselves that 'inalienable right'. This is the 'moral universe' that Martin Luther King Junior understood.

The growth of the Church in the south is also remarkable. In the 1990s the Khartoum Government called for jihad against the south but Islam has not made much (if any) progress. Villages which previously were ruled by Sharia Law now do not even have a mosque. Unlike almost everywhere else I have been in Africa, I have never met a fellowship of Muslims in southern Sudan[5].

I asked one man why he was a Christian, and he said, 'Well – I grew up in an Islamic school, I was forced to learn the Koran, but I looked at Muslims and I have seen them decapitate some of my brothers and so I chose to be a Christian as it was a religion my parents practised.'

Whilst I have been amazed and humbled by the faith of

the southern Sudanese many times – it is also fair to say that many take to Christianity in rebellion against the northern Government. Some claim it as much as a political banner as a heartfelt conviction that Christ is Lord.

That said, the church represents one of the few institutions which has remained and even grown during the war. Everywhere I have been in southern Sudan, the largest building is the church. I awoke one morning in a village called Nyadin, a village without road access, without phone access, without even a recognisable shop, surrounded by swamps and marsh. And yet on this Sunday morning half the town seemed to be marching behind a banner of the cross. They trooped up and down the airstrip before entering the church and beginning a service. In Padak, a place that witnessed bombings and massacres, there was a very large church filled every Sunday. On an assessment to Omdurman, a place miles north of any NGO or Western influence, raided regularly by militia, I awoke to the sound of church singing at 6.00 a.m. – a sound so tuneful it seemed to breeze into and sweeten my early morning thoughts and dreams. At times I was amazed by the faith and commitment of the population barely able to feed themselves, yet prepared to build a structure which in their setting was truly colossal. All of these churches are without the Western missionaries or recent Western influence. Maybe God's grace is sufficient?

So – hope for Sudan? Well, it will take time, decades even – but God has not forgotten her. A Sudanese preacher spoke on Psalm 25 with the following message for the assembled worshippers:

Brothers and sisters, the Psalmist says, 'To you, O Lord, I lift up my heart'. This today is the prayer of all Christians of all denominations in the Sudan and all Christians all over the world.... Let us stand firm because he is with us...we don't resist with stones or guns. Our weapon as Christians is the sword of the Spirit, the Holy Bible and Prayer.....

I don't want to say bad things, but I must say this: our Lord is powerful. Can anyone tell me of a Christian who took a bulldozer to knock down schools or mosques anywhere? Brothers and sisters in the Government – do something to make sure our schools and places of worship are not destroyed. We also assure the Government that we won't take up stones or guns to defend our schools or churches.

We know God is in us. We don't fear those who can kill the body. We fear those who can kill the body and the soul. Continue praying until this issue is resolved. We believe God has a purpose in allowing this to happen at this time. It is for the good of Christians in this country.

Some people dream of wiping out the Christian faith by the end of the decade. They are entitled to their dream. Let them continue to dream. I have a different dream that the people of Sudan will soon live together in peace and harmony. I have a dream that all the people of the Sudan will be worshipping the one God, the Lord Jesus Christ, by the end of the next hundred years. I have a dream that the Wali and Turabi, will be the leading apostles bringing the gospel of the Lord Jesus Christ to the people. Are you ready to dream with me?[6]

First Trip into Sudan: Welcome Back to Sudan

Fergus, the Programme Director, and I flew into Nyadien, my first trip back to Sudan. We met some of the locals including a sparkling 60-year-old Italian priest living with the Nuer tribe. He had no possessions other than a mosquito net, sleeping mat and eating bowl. He walked where they walked, traversing swamps and crossing miles of pasture land; he ate what they ate (an unvaried diet of sorghum meals and milk) and he slept where they slept (on a mat in a hut). When a place was attacked he fled with them. He was loved by the Nuer. He introduced us to some locals and knew their names and family backgrounds. He clearly had a sharp mind, spoke their language and spoke of his love for the Nuer but was also perfectly willing to talk about their faults. More than anyone I have met, he seemed to achieve the balance of loving the people and hating their sin. A few long-term missionaries seem to have become a bit disillusioned or even embittered by their struggles. Not so this man, who has spent many years among the Sudanese with barely a break. After over an hour sitting on the floor in his empty hut we came away knowing we had met a man of God (and massively mauled by mosquitoes).

The flight to take us out of there was due in at 10.00 a.m. the next morning and by eleven o'clock we wondered what had caused the delay. Eventually, we discovered that the Government had declared a ten-day flight ban over Eastern Equatoria (the most southerly and eastern region of Sudan) which stood between us and home. No Sudan-bound flights were to take off from Lokichoggio for ten days. The Government wanted the airspace so they could bomb the Sudan People's Liberation Army (SPLA)[7] who had recently captured a town.

Fergus already had over 160 mosquito bites on his back and by 7.00 each evening we were wrapped up in our mosquito nets, such was the number of insects. The thought of spending another ten days here did not appeal.

There was one UN security plane in the area and mercifully it collected us the next day. It was on a routine surveillance and reconnaissance flight, and after picking us up it flew about 10 metres above the ground. We asked why we were flying so low wondering whether it had anything to do with evading radars. 'No, it is just more fun', replied Stefano the security officer. We headed off west to the oil fields and could see where the rigs had been. In order to dig for oil, the Government needed unrestricted access, something the locals and the SPLA were keen not to provide. In a process euphemistically termed a 'scorched earth policy' the Government erased all traces of human life and built a road through the swamp to enable drilling on the oil fields. Eighteen months before, I had interviewed Nuers who had fled the area we were now flying over; they recounted horrors of gunship attacks followed by infantry assaults. These successful attacks meant the Government was free to build a road, which was vital to support the drilling operation. We followed that asphalt road south and then onto Rumbek, where we would see out the remainder of our ten days.

It turned out that the head of the World Food Programme was also stuck in Sudan and he was far too important to be left there for ten days. The UN organised a plane to fly him out. Somehow, thankfully, we also managed to get on that plane. In order to circumnavigate the no-fly zone, we were forced to fly into Ethiopian airspace before landing back safely in Lokichoggio.

Ayod and the Football Match

In the early 1990s Ayod was the centre of fighting between the Nuer and Dinka. Riek Machar, the Nuer commander, had temporarily used it as a military base. Deborah Scroggins described it as one corner of a 'hunger triangle' with malnutrition rates 'among the highest ever recorded'.[8] In 1993 a tit-for-tat battle over the town saw Garang's (the leader of the SPLA and in this instance Dinka) forces take the town before Riek's forces recaptured it a few days later. On returning 'they found that Garang's men had razed the town and burned down the feeding centre, incinerating more than 100 people inside. The bodies of 200 other people lay sprawled about the charred remains of the village.'[9] Garang attacked again, about ten days later, with a series of mortar rounds and grenades hitting the feeding centre and clinic which contained about 1,600 people. Nugent, an observer, wrote of the latest attack that 'the foetor of burning flesh and hair engulfs us...I stare at the aid station as war transforms it into a crematorium.'[10] When Garang's troops had retreated, Riek and Nugent walked from Waat to Ayod and found the remains of dead people in every village, mostly women, sometimes split in half by machetes. 'Often the women's killers had spread their legs and inserted sticks into their vaginas.'[11]

Nearly ten years later, Roselyn (the Tearfund nutritionist) and I, following reports that the humanitarian situation was bad (again), arrived in the town to conduct a rapid nutritional assessment. From the airstrip to the camp was about a three minute walk. In that time two things struck us: firstly we were here in the middle of nowhere but it had evidently once been a 'somewhere'. In Sudan there are virtually no buildings, no cement, no walls, no tin roofs, every building is a mud hut. In Ayod remnants of high brick buildings, broken down water pumps, frames of large warehouses all bore evidence to the fact that Ayod was once 'something'. Dead bodies are buried and not seen; destroyed buildings remain and point to a more prosperous past, reminding you of what might have been. Ten years since the worst fighting little or nothing had been done to develop the town. It still had not recovered from the war; it still seemed to be in a state of shock and dereliction.

The second thing that struck us was that this was very obviously not much more than a military camp. The tukuls (mud huts) were ordered and lined in a way never seen in a 'normal' town or village, the population was predominantly young men. You rarely see young men as they are either with the military or looking after cattle; in a nomadic society the women with children and the elderly tend to be the ones who stay at home. In Ayod there were some women but they seemed only to be there to help out with the cooking. My heart sank as there was no way we were going to do a humanitarian intervention in a military barracks and yet we would still have to complete an assessment.

We trained locals in how to collect data and went out to find 100 children to measure their weight and height. In total we found 27, hardly evidence of a normal African village where it is generally regarded that 20 per cent will be under five. So I walked around the place and soon found some impressive artillery. The old school was now filled with ammunition, and nearby stood a few land-to-air missile launchers. On the airstrip was a broken down plane, which we discovered had been used to fly people to the front line. The SPLA had recently captured a town called Torit and were fighting hard to maintain it against a determined Government attack. The plane on the runway had evidently been hired, in desperation, to get rebel troops from this region as fast as possible to defend the hapless Torit. Those troops were mostly bomb fodder and probably now six feet under as the Government used their considerable air assets to obliterate their enemy and win back the town. The guys with me now were the lucky ones who remained behind.

As the large African sun was setting, easing the heat and dulling the colours on the horizon from sharp blues to pastel reds, I joined in a game of football. Such games ease the boredom of the late afternoon; I also enjoy them because generally I have had more exposure to the game of football than the average opponent from rural Sudan and therefore tend to be able to hold my own. Tonight I was not holding back – going into tackles full on, charging up and down the pitch in an effort to get rid of some latent frustration. After ten minutes I stopped, looked up, stared around me and took in the scene. All the men I was playing with were wearing khaki trousers, and at least three of the six spectators were supplementing their khaki outfit with a hefty AK-47. It suddenly struck me I was playing football with a bona fide bunch of rebel African soldiers, in a military barracks, in the middle of absolutely nowhere. I no longer found it necessary to play quite so hard.

Death, Love, Anger and Justice

It was the first time I had seen the feeding programme since it had fully opened. Within five minutes of arriving at Tierraliet, in Aweil South, Bhar el Ghazal, we entered the therapeutic feeding ward. The numbers of children arriving in the programme were massive. In the first few weeks over 600 severely malnourished children (in addition to hundreds of moderately malnourished) were admitted. The worst cases of the severely malnourished were referred to this in-patient feeding centre. Between twenty and thirty children in the worst state you could imagine a human child to be in, lay there – highly malnourished, disease ridden, with fragile hip bones, ribs and shoulder blades protruding. You did not have to be a doctor to realise they were on the very edge of existence. Life was at its most vulnerable while death, inches away, seemed to stalk every child in the recently constructed mud ward.

I came out of there in shock; lost and off-balance as though whacked over the head. Taddy, a nurse with years of experience in feeding programmes, could barely control herself either and we shared a quiet moment of prayer as we were so disorientated.

There were two children the nurses were really worried about; death seemed to be opening its jaws and we desperately wanted to overcome it. Before we went to bed we prayed for them. I awoke early the next morning. The nurses, who had barely slept, were in the feeding centre. Both children had died during the night – 'that simple, frictionless, motionless deliverance from a state of half-life to death itself'.[12] I didn't know what to say and wandered around the feeding centre wondering what to do. The grieving mothers wrapped their deceased children in a blanket and lay by them, gathering strength ahead of their long walk home. They seemed to know instinctively what to do and acted with enormous dignity and calm.

I returned to my tent and as I passed Concepta the nurse, I tried to offer some words of encouragement; instead I found my cheeks wobble, my bottom lip fall away and I blubbed it. I looked up and saw Concepta's beautiful Kenyan, deer-like eyes, staring back at me, slightly bemused and probably thinking I was a bit strange. I did not expect myself to react like this, and was embarrassed. It was not my first encounter with death and on previous occasions I had maintained control. However it had been a long week: under mortar fire in Padak, vehicles stuck in Malualkon with people walking 13 kilometres home during the night; a store roof had collapsed in Rumbek, food had run out in Aweil South and medicines were sent to the wrong location in Oriny. Each event had stripped away my normal defence systems and peeled away, layer by layer, my outer shell.

After my failed conversation, I took myself off for a shower. I stood there, under the bucket, staring up at the sky and through my sobbing cried out, 'It is not fair. It simply is not fair that a child should die because his mother cannot find two meals in a day. It is not fair that she has to walk eight hours to find any semblance of medical care. This world, Lord, is simply not fair.' After so long in the job, it was encouraging, tired as I was, to see I still had a heart and that underneath it all it did still hurt me. But along with compassion, had come anger. To my surprise it was anger which was welling up, anger that we should live in a world where such enormous riches do not reach these people in Sudan. Anger that whilst mankind has achieved so much, still children die from a lack of the most basic of needs. Anger, that in my country I could stuff my face each day whilst here people were starving.

Love and anger are the different sides to the same coin. As we love the hungry, so too we find anger about the conditions, systems and structures which made them hungry. If you love your son, you would become angry if someone bullied him. The greater the negative effects of the bullying, the stronger your anger becomes. The more you love that child the stronger your anger would be. The anger flows from your love of the child. God too, shares that anger. Because he loves everyone, he too becomes angry when they are bullied or sinned against. He must do. His love would not be genuine otherwise. This anger comes through in the Bible: injustice is mentioned over 120 times in the Old Testament. Jesus shared and exhibited that anger. He twice turned the tables in the marketplace, passionate about the injustices committed there. He spoke out to those in power: 'Woe to you Pharisees, because you...neglect justice and the love of God.'[13] Clearly God's love and justice were linked and as Jesus was full of God's love, he could not help but be angered by sin.

The church I grew up in taught me well that God's heart is to have compassion on the poor. I believe the church is generous in its compassionate giving for the poor. It is good at seeing a starving child and recognising that a godly response is to try to get that child food. Perhaps we are less good at seeing the systems and structures which have forced that child into poverty and then once we have seen those injustices to be angry about them with a holy passion.

In all my years at church I cannot remember a single sermon on justice. In Christian circles you are more likely to meet discussions on different denominational styles of worship, homosexuality or the Toronto Blessing than you are how to fight the many injustices that are at the heart of our world. Yet it is a central facet of God's heart, it was a central facet of Jesus' ministry: 'The Spirit of the Lord is on me, because he has anointed me to preach good news to the poor. He has sent me to proclaim freedom for the prisoners and...to release the oppressed.'[14]

Would Paul be able to write to us, as he did the Corinthians, 'See what this Godly sorrow has produced in you: what earnestness...what concern, *what readiness to see justice done*' [my emphasis]?[15] If Jesus spoke to the church in the West, would he need to change his words spoken to the teachers of the law: 'But you have neglected the more important matters of the law – justice, mercy and faithfulness?'[16]

December 2003 – A Trip on Lake Turkana

It was nearing the end of the year and we were driving out of Lokichoggio to Lake Turkana in northern Kenya for a three day break.

The roads, were fast and empty, the scenery a majestic, semi-desert terrain – with shimmering green shrubs and soft yellow sands outstretched underneath rectilinear mountains in the hazy distance. En route we stopped the car and stood in silence listening to the sound of nothing. No humans, no vehicles, no animals, no machines.

We arrived at Kolokal, a town at the end of the road

next to Lake Turkana and then drove around the lagoon through the sanddunes. After getting stuck a couple of times we arrived at our destination.

The manager had already prepared the boat. In a matter of minutes we had paid up, repacked our bags and were off. This was efficiency that any hotel would be proud of. The tiny glimmering waves were reflecting the shining sun and work was far away.

There were seven of us on the trip – three Norwegians (so lots of Viking jokes as we crossed the water), one French, one Swiss, myself and Rachel (now my fiancée). We also had someone steering the boat and a guide; making a total of nine. A notice on the boat read 'maximum passengers six' – but we were on holiday, health and safety was something we had left behind.

Forty minutes after leaving we arrived and were the only humans on Central Island. I had seen it before from the air – a small volcanic island, with high peaks and three lakes. Walking onto the island, as the sole human inhabitants, was breathtaking. The place felt enchanted. It was the nearest I had been to the garden of Eden. Every minute a different flock of birds flew imperiously overhead; as we walked through the undergrowth, giant crickets landed on our arms. We arrived at the first lake on the island and could make out the eyes of crocodiles and then as we climbed up the hill were able to discern their shape traversing the lake with their heads out of the water and their bodies just under. This is what the ancient Celtics termed a 'thin veil' – the distinction between heaven and earth felt slim on Central Island.

We set up camp. Fish with rice was our meal, we chatted, saw off a bottle of wine and went to sleep at around 9.00 p.m.

We awoke, had a light breakfast and walked off to explore the rest of the island: high peaks, narrow escarpments, long cliff faces, more birdlife. As the island was an active volcano in some areas, the rock was steaming with hot sulphur, and two of the lakes were a lime green in colour[17]. We got back to base at 12.00 midday and with little food left we were all keen to return to the mainland and have a good night's sleep at the hotel. Lake Turkana is one of the lowest spots on the continent of Africa, it is in the middle of a desert and at midday it gets hot.

At one o'clock we boarded the boat and set off on our nine-kilometre journey to the mainland. It was windy and the waves were higher than the day before. A few waves rocked the boat, and Gabby got a bit concerned about her bags getting wet – but this was all 'par for the course' on a such a trip. As we got further into the lake, the waves got bigger, they rocked the boat harder and were soon spilling over the top. I was sitting at the back and saw panic on people's faces, then a wave crashed over my side. Now we were bailing out fast, instructing the guide to head back and throwing our belongings overboard. As we began changing our direction another wave hit our stern. The water was sloshing around our shins and the boat was lowering in the water. We were rapidly sinking. An order was given and out we all jumped. As we did so, the boat flipped and capsized. We had been on the water for twenty minutes, and were about 3 kilometres from the island, 6 kilometres from the mainland. At this point our guide, in broken English, informed us he could not swim; then the other guide did the same. Alongside the capsized boat, there were nine of us, two were non-swimmers and we had six life jackets.

After we agreed the island was nearer we began pushing the boat back to shore, with seven of us swimming and two on top of the capsized boat, paddling.

The major fear was that we would drift down lake and out of reach of the island but thankfully there was no current. For an hour or more we definitely made good progress. The island was getting bigger, jokes were being cracked and spirits were high. Then the waves became bigger and rather than flowing perpendicular to our direction, as before, they were hitting us straight on. The boat became lower in the water and any yards made were soon knocked back by the waves. We found one of our abandoned floating tents and tried to use it as a sail...it didn't work.

We reckoned we were now about a kilometre from shore, and not making progress. The idea was suggested that the swimmers left the boat (leaving the non-swimmers afloat on top of it) and made it to shore where some sailors had just arrived and they could come out and rescue the other two. I was initially against the idea – two golden rules I had in my head were never leave the boat and never split the party. After a while of deliberating – Rachel swam past the boat to prove it would be more effective to swim and the two non-swimmers also urged us to go ahead.

So seven of us left both non-swimmers on the boat and began the swim to the island. We had now been in the water two hours. The waves were large, the shore seemed a long distance away. After a while, it was obvious we were making progress and with no current, I knew we would make it to shore. It would take a long time and none of us had swum that far before but there was collective relief as we realised that we would survive. A few people mentioned the crocodiles but we tried not to think of that. (Lake Turkana contains more crocodiles than any other lake in Africa). Thankfully the fishermen from further down the island had seen us before we reached the island and came to rescue us. We all made it to shore. I was wearing a T-shirt which had rubbed against my skin causing both nipples to bleed. My suggestion that they be kissed better was not met with enthusiasm by Rachel.

It was 4.20 p.m. when we landed; we had been in the water for over three hours. Our boat was left to drift in the lake. Since our last meal we had taken a four-hour walk and now a three-hour swim. It would soon get dark and we had no food. We dried our clothes, set up makeshift shelters and with nothing else to do we slept. The next morning the wind and waves were down and we crossed safely over to the mainland in the same boats which had rescued us, accompanied by a double rainbow on the horizon. We landed and were met by the hotel manager who seemed only to care about his lost boat. We walked for forty-five minutes back to the lodge, ate, got in the car and began our journey home. We got stuck in the mud for one hour and just made it to Kakuma in time for our escort back to Lokichoggio. In three days we had had only three decent meals, eight hours of exercise and ten hours of travel either by boat or car.

In the closing minutes before the boat turned, I had said one prayer: 'I don't care about any other belongings, Lord, but I do not want to lose my Bible.' It was my most treasured possession. Given to me at the age of thirteen, it had been my constant companion, and had travelled with me almost every day of my life since. I had underlined all my favourite verses and kept many memorabilia, notes and touching letters inside it. When I got back to the island – I said 'Lord, well you have rescued me and everyone of us – I cannot possibly complain about a Bible.'

Three days after we got back we received a phone call from the Kenya Wildlife Service office in a town 50 kilometres from the lake. The man on the end of the phone said he had been handed a bag and thought it was probably mine. Somehow the wind had pushed the boat, with our rucksack (which had apparently floated underneath) 8 kilometres across the lake and 20 kilometres south where it moored on the shore. Hardly anyone lived on the lake, even fewer have access to a vehicle. The people that found it had the honesty and ability to transport it 50 kilometres to the nearest town. Inside the bag was my Bible, still readable.

Leaving Sudan

In March 2004, after eighteen months of working in southern Sudan, I returned to the UK. I had left a job I loved, and to which I had given so much, to be in England with neither a job or a permanent place to live. While being in the UK is great fun, there was the odd symptom which hinted that, at a deeper level, it was a difficult readjustment. On Easter Sunday I was asked to talk to a bunch of middle-class Christians from Cambridgeshire on 'Where is the risen Christ in Sudan?' Coming as this did, so soon after my assignment, with my perspective so filled and absorbed with the southern Sudanese problems, troubles and difficulties, I found it almost impossible to think of anything positive to say. So, through an embarrassing amount of tears, basically said that I had no idea where Christ was in southern Sudan. I am not sure any of those listening, nor myself, quite knew what to make of what I shared.

By the summer the wedding preparations were finalized, and on 19 June Rachel and I married in Hampshire, near her family home. Standing in the church, surrounded by friends and family who had been such a faithful support to us over many long months overseas, and seeing Rachel walk down the aisle grinning from ear to ear, was one of the happiest and most emotional moments of my life.

Around the same time Tearfund was launching a response to the Darfur crisis which was hitting the headlines. On our honeymoon we watched CNN footage of the disaster and in January 2005, Rachel and I went to be a part of the response. Living in Khartoum we worked with the teams responding to the Darfur crisis. At the time of writing the final draft of this book, it is over two and a half years later and we are still there, accompanied now by our daughter Iona.

Notes

1. In 'quantifying genocide' arrived at 500,000 dead in 1988 in 'Quantifying genocide in the Southern Sudan 1983 – 1993. Quoted in Deborah Scroggins, *Emma's War*, HarperCollins, 2004.
2. Kala-azar is a wasting disease that if untreated will almost certainly kill.
3. Quoted in Deborah Scroggins, *Emma's War*, HarperCollins, 2004, page 207.
4. Clayborne Carson, *Autobiography of Martin Luther King Junior*, Warner, 1999.

5. (They do exist in towns formerly held by the government, but at the time of writing I had never been to one.)

6. From Simon Guillebaud, *For What It's Worth*, Monarch Books, 2006, pages 149–50.

7. The major rebel group fighting the northern government.

8. From Deborah Scroggins, *Emma's War*, HarperCollins, 2004 – quoting the US centres for disease control.

9. Deborah Scroggins, *Emma's War*, HarperCollins, 2004.

10. Quoted in Deborah Scroggins, *Emma's War*, HarperCollins, 2004.

11. Deborah Scroggins, *Emma's War*, HarperCollins, 2004.

12. George Alagiah, *A Passage to Africa*, Time Warner, 2002.

13. Luke 11:42.

14. Luke 4:18.

15. 2 Corinthians 7:11.

16. Matthew 23:23.

17. As a result of run-off from the lava flows, the lake's waters are mildly alkaline, enough to give the water a slightly slimy, soapy feel. This does not prevent life, as fresh water from Ethiopia's Omo River – the lake's only perennially-flowing inlet – dilutes the waters.

CHAPTER SEVEN

Stepping into the North and Darfur

Consciously and unconsciously, I had preconceived notions, images and prejudices about the north. Viewed from southern Sudan, Khartoum was the abode of the devil incarnate, the bastion of power which had inflicted dozens of years of war on southern Sudan, mercilessly destroyed villages and sent bombers and gunships to kill and maim. Only a small percentage of the population were controlling the war but perhaps a large number of families had sent their troops to fight, inspired, surely, by the holy jihad of Islam? Khartoum was, after all, the major market, creating a demand for slaves? The Government had supported Osama Bin Laden in the mid-1990s and the reason I was here now was because it had turned its bloody hands on Darfur.

These were some of the perceptions I carried as I first arrived in Khartoum, the capital of Sudan, more than four years after first setting foot in the country. You cannot understand a country without visiting the capital and I had built up my own preconceptions about Khartoum. A bit like hearing about someone before you meet them, I found many of my self-developed views were wrong. I expected almost everyone, and especially those in Government and Government administration, to be against southerners. So it was a surprise when the first

Government official I met at passport control, turned out to be a southerner.

Living in the south you find yourself, knowingly and unknowingly, supporting their 'cause' and therefore those from the north represented the enemy. 'GoS (Government of Sudan) Soldier' was a phrase I had read in dozens of security reports and was therefore synonymous in my mind with some crazed lunatic bent on killing 'innocent' southerners. Within a few hours of being in Khartoum I set eyes, for the first time, on a 'GoS soldier'. There were no horns on his head and to my amazement his skin colour was more black (akin to the African southerners) than brown (akin to the more 'Arab' northerners). As I stared at him, it became clear he was just an ordinary young man – no different from some of my friends who had joined the British army and been sent to Northern Ireland.

Early on I sat down with El Hadi who worked in the Tearfund office in Khartoum. As we were chatting about Sudan and his background it suddenly occurred to me which tribe he was from: 'So you must be a Baggara?' I asked. The Baggara, for years, had been armed by the Government to loot, pillage and burn villages in Bhar el Ghazel where I had worked in the south.

'Yes,' came the innocent reply.

Involuntarily something jumped and twisted inside me – a part of my spirit had been repulsed. Without real-izing it I had absorbed a prejudice against this tribe and projected it onto this man. El Hadi was a nice, balanced Muslim and we developed a strong working relationship, he later welcomed me to his home and introduced me to his family. But if I, with only a few years association with the south, found such feelings in me, how much deeper would they run had it been my village laid waste, my wife raped, my child abducted? If all I had known, grown up with and feared was this man's tribe, the feeling would surely have been a thousand times stronger. No wonder tribal distrust runs deep.

And so over the weeks and months, I found myself reassessing my opinion of Khartoum and the people of north Sudan. I ate in their houses, met their children, worked with them and they became my friends.

The World's Worst Humanitarian Crisis

There was a general consensus that it was the 'world's worst humanitarian crisis', as labelled by the UN. Former UN Humanitarian Coordinator for Sudan Dr Makesh Kabila also described it as a 'historically unprecedented humanitarian and human rights catastrophe'. The scale and speed of destruction preceding the humanitarian crisis surprised most of the world.

Darfur is in western Sudan. It is the size of France with a population less than Paris (6 million). In a matter of months 2 million people (one third) had been forced from their homes and were living in camps; 200,000 of them were in Chad. Estimates of the number dead vary from 180,000 to far more. Imagine driving from London to Edinburgh and then down to Cardiff before returning to London and seeing every single village en route obliterated. Viewing Darfur from the air, the ground is littered with brown rings, marking former homes – now burnt to nothing. Hundreds of villages were destroyed, many of the surviving villages have done so only on account of protection money paid to their would-be destroyers. In military terms it was a highly sophisticated, thorough and organized campaign. Arranging the logistics, airpower, and coordination of troops for such an operation requires both the military strength and the coordinated support of the Sudanese Government. As you drive through Darfur you see village after village, hut after hut in ruins; often only cooking pots remain on the floor, evidence people did not even have time to collect their most basic of items before fleeing or being killed.

The majority of the destruction occurred before the international community arrived in force. In part this is because the Government did a good job of preventing the outside world from seeing what was happening. They have created a network of bureaucratic offices, intertwined with a complicated system of numerous visas, travel permits and area permits which block access. Meanwhile the peace process, occurring in the south, was nearing its final stages after years of hard work. Getting this signed off was the international community's priority and the majority of diplomatic 'carrot and stick' resources were focused on this. The Government knew this, and strung out negotiations for as long as it took to 'finish the job' in Darfur. By June 2004, when the majority of aid agencies arrived in Darfur, the damage had largely been done.[1]

The history to the Darfur conflict is long and complex; many argue it had been going on for years before, but February 2003 sparked the most horrendous fighting, the like of which Darfur had never before seen. (Much of the fighting coincided with the Iraq war when international attention was elsewhere.)

Coexisting in Darfur, as with many areas of Africa, there are nomadic pastoralists (using land for grazing cattle and camels) and sedentary farmers (who use land predominantly for arable farming). Sporadic tensions between these groups had existed for as long as they had both been in Darfur; but the predominant relationship had, historically, been one of mutual respect and relative harmony as they synchronized their livelihoods. Very broadly (but not exclusively) the sedentary farmers tended to be more 'African' in identity and the pastoralists more 'Arab', though those terms are relatively new ones in their consciousness (intermarriage has always been common) as they have now become politicized.

In the years preceding 2003, unseen by most political observers, Darfur was a cauldron of factors steadily heading towards a ferocious boiling point: Arab supremacist agendas, political marginalization, depleted environmental resources and population increases which fed land conflict all combined to marginalize and frustrate Darfurians giving rise to the formation of the Sudan Liberation Army (SLA). The SLA rebel group represented the largest African (and some Arab) tribes in Darfur. Recognizing that the imminent peace in the south and subsequent power to the SPLA had come through the gun while their more diplomatic efforts had resulted in virtually no political gain, the SLA leadership took to arms. In a series of strategic strikes they hit key Government positions before disappearing into the bush. Winning most of their initial engagements, their popularity amongst the Darfurians grew and soon the Justice and Equity Movement (JEM), a more national and Islamic rebel group, joined their cause.

In the early months the Government struggled to over-come the rebellion. The security cabal at the heart of the Government were unhappy about the political losses involved in the southern peace negotiations, and as a form of appeasement were handed the 'Darfur file'. With the world's eyes on the southern peace process, they attempted to utterly obliterate their Darfurian enemy, unleashing enormous force, arming Arab militias, mobilizing their own Popular Defence Forces (PDF), utilizing considerable air assets to bomb and attack villages before the ground troops followed up to ensure the villages remained 'empty'.

The statistics are huge: over 2 million forced from their homes, with tens of thousands of people killed. Some 'Arab' forces attempted to 'dilute' the African tribes by raping thousands of women. Many young girls were impregnated thereby giving birth to 'Arab' children; other women were sexually mutilated and still others stabbed in the vagina to ensure they could never conceive or were 'socially unclean' for marriage. Once in the relative safety of camps the oppressed people were terrorized. Regular rapes, beatings or killings are enough to maintain the fear in a population and keep them too scared to return to their land. At the time of writing they have remained in their camps for more than three years. It is hard to imagine them feeling safe enough to leave.

The world began to notice and it became regular news by April 2004; by June a large number of agencies were allowed in to provide the humanitarian response. With millions forced to miss planting seasons and living in camps the humanitarian situation was terrible. The African Union was tasked with monitoring fragile ceasefire agreements; Tearfund were among the first wave of agencies into Darfur and have been providing water, sanitation, health education, food to malnourished children and recovery agriculture to thousands of families. We have also been heavily involved in advocating for justice and peace for Darfur, with opportunities to speak and meet a variety of politicians, diplomats and UN workers including fifteen members of the security council.

This crisis, unlike that of southern Sudan, does not have a religious element to it. Darfur is an almost exclusively Muslim state. The Government is Muslim, the rebels are, if anything, Muslims, the displaced are Muslim, the raped and the dead are Muslims too. Operation World describes Darfur as one of the least evangelized corners of the earth. Unlike almost everywhere else I had been in Africa there was virtually no church. Where it existed, it was very small, started either through displaced Dinka or other southerners working in Darfur. Whilst I was often touched by the reverence and devotion of Muslims in Darfur, on other occasions I also found myself aware of a spiritual heaviness. I am not normally sensitive to such things, but some villages, which had witnessed so much killing and remained riddled with military and guns, felt as though they were the heart of darkness.

After eighteen months of working and living in Darfur and Khartoum, Rachel heard a sermon on Jesus as the water of life and said afterwards she felt almost completely dry spiritually. I shared this with some of my friends who were not Christian and to my surprise they totally understood. 'Yes,' they replied, 'Spiritually speaking Khartoum is a very tough place to live.'

As she listened to the sermon about Jesus being the water of life, Rachel reflected on all the water points we had provided in Darfur. I am certain that God can use the crisis to bring his living water to Darfur. He did not create the war, that was done by man; but he can use the crisis for good. Tearfund are not there to preach in words; we are there to bring assistance to those in need. I do believe, however, that Tearfund are the front end of the gospel in Darfur, able to manifest God's love to thousands of people. Trusting that Christ is in us and guiding us, we can be his footprints (however faint) and his presence across the land.

The rebels initially listed lack of good governance as a major reason for their uprising. Reading Ezekiel 34 and applying it to the Darfur situation gave me encouragement.

> [My sheep] were scattered because there was no shepherd, and when they were scattered they became food for all the wild animals. My sheep wandered over all the mountains and on every high hill. (Ezekiel 34:5,6)

When the sheep are lost or stuck they begin to bleat. Maybe the Darfur crisis is the first echo of their bleating. Maybe we represent the first steps of Jesus on a long walk to reclaim his sheep.

> As surely as I live, declares the Sovereign Lord, because my flock lacks a shepherd...I will rescue my flock...I myself will search for my sheep and look after them....I will search for the lost and bring back the strays.   (Ezekiel 34:8,10,11,16)

Maybe he will use aid agencies to bring relief.

> I will rescue them...I myself will tend my sheep...I will bind up the injured and strengthen the weak...they will no longer be victims of famine.
>
> (Ezekiel 34:12,15,16,29)

Was Darfur a genocide? Should there be an international criminal court?

> You have ruled them harshly and brutally...I will hold them accountable for my flock...I will judge between the fat sheep and the lean sheep... They will know that I am the Lord, when I break the bars of their yoke and rescue them from the hands of those who enslaved them.
>
> (Ezekiel 34:4,10,20,27)

The first conflict in the Bible, between Cain and Abel, was between pastoralists and arable farmers. So too the one in Darfur. Maybe God will restore prosperity to both forms of livelihood.

> ...I will pasture them on the mountains... There they will lie down in good grazing land... The trees of the field will yield their fruit and the ground will yield its crops... I will provide for them a land renowned for its crops.
>
> (Ezekiel 34:13,14,27–29)

(Note this applies to pastoralists and arable farmers.) Can there ever be a peace out of this almighty mess? Can they ever coexist?

> I will make a covenant of peace with them...I will bless them...they will live in safety and no one will make them afraid.   (Ezekiel 34:25,26,28)

Rachel and I lived in Khartoum working for the Darfur programme for over two and a half years. Darfurians are a long, long way from 'living in safety' where 'no one will make them afraid'. If we are to see a covenant of peace and the different livelihoods coexisting we need to be thinking in years, maybe decades, rather than months. The wounds of this current crisis run too deep and the political landscape is too fractious for anything else to be possible. Finding even tiny hints of progress is difficult; macro and micro peace initiatives need to work together and progress on both is slim at best. For aid agencies it was a highly dangerous environment – Tearfund had staff attacked, beaten, abused, taken hostage, held at gunpoint and killed.

Whether it is compassion at the absolute poverty, anger at the oppressed millions, fear over the insecurity, sadness at the loss of life, despair over the future, or stress because of the work required, Darfur takes you right to the edge of your emotions. It seems to push you further than you have been before.

The Death of John Garang

John Garang was the leader of the southern Sudanese rebellion movement (the SPLA/M). After twenty-two years of fighting he was appointed into the Islamic Government as First Vice President, the first southerner and the first non-Muslim to hold such a rank since independence. He was sworn in on 9 July 2005; it was an historic event comparable to Nelson Mandela's inauguration and the streets of Khartoum were alive with southerners celebrating.

Not three weeks after his inauguration however, John Garang died in a helicopter crash; the news broke on Monday morning. The call on Wednesday brought more bad news: Matiep (another ex-rebel Nuer leader, formerly opposed to Garang) had been killed in the riots. True or not this rumour would further enflame Khartoum which had already been trashed in riots over the past two days.

I was having lunch with a friend when I heard. We went on to his roof to have a look: smoke billowed in the distance, cars were hooting, shops were quickly boarding up, almost every person and every vehicle was rushing away from town.

I was soon down the stairs and into my car. I drove off down a side street. People and cars sped past. I called Rita (an American colleague), she was fine and in the office. Nicole was at home having a day off. Salafa and Amthal, our only national staff who had made it in to the office, had already left to get home as fast as possible. 'Where's Rach?' I asked. 'She is out buying lunch.'

I tried to call Rachel – no answer. Now I was onto Cemetery Road and things were clearly heating up; people were panicking. The people were moving in the direction of the office. I called Rita again, saying 'Pack up the computers, we are heading to Ryad.'

Was Rachel OK? I tried her again – it was only a few minutes since my first attempt but it was long enough to worry, long enough for my emotions to run high, long enough for my heart to thump, my blood to start pounding, long enough to catch a tiny glimpse of how thousands of mothers, husbands, wives, lovers were feeling now (or would feel in countless other riot or war situations), utterly unaware of the whereabouts of their loved ones. Rachel picked up the phone; she was on Street Fifteen.

'Ed, things are happening here...'

'Get to the Ryad flats. We're evacuating the office. I'll meet you there.'

'OK...'

I knew she understood and would know what to do. My worry subsided.

As I pulled into the street where our office was located, I saw Amthal, our loyal and motherly secretary clearly in a state of distress. She had to get through town to go home, every car was heading in the other direction and no one would give her a lift. I told her it was best to come with us. She could stay the night there and at least she would be safe. She called her son to let him know. We cleared the office, took the satellite phone and headed home. I made a mental check of all the staff – everyone was accounted for except Salafa. We called her up and she had made it back safely.

We got home to the flat and bunked up. I was amazed how fast the adrenalin could flow and how tired it had left me – a tiny taste of both the fear and fatigue of fighting.

It turned out the rumour was false, Matiep had not been killed. Had it been true, the results would have been unthinkable. Garang's death had opened up old suspicions, and prejudices. Southerners believed the helicopter crash was orchestrated by the Government, who had fought them for decades, and was now, again, showing its true colours. These suspicions ignited the city which erupted along deep and old fault lines, allowing the latent lava of anger and distrust to flow over into riots that smashed almost every shop in the centre of town. Southerners, so long tamed by the iron fist of the police state, rose up and gave vent to their inner feelings. In response, many imams did the same and called for retaliation – some even called it a holy jihad. The pendulum of violence was gathering momentum, people gathered in the early hours of Wednesday morning and had it not been for a divinely timed thunderstorm, which drenched and immobilized the city, it might have swung still higher. For some Muslims the crash had been a hand of God, confirmation that an infidel should never be allowed to rule them, that God was against the peace agreement which had ousted shariah law and this was their chance to gain political mileage.

Matiep was a Nuer, he had also fought Garang for many years. His death would have opened the bloody Nuer – Dinka clashes which had raged for much of the 90s. The whole country could have fallen to bits along the seams.

Thankfully, Matiep was soon on TV, appealing for calm, as had the president and the new leader of the SPLA. Add this to the large numbers of riot police quelling the violence and the riot's flames soon turned to embers and calm returned to Khartoum. The crash, it turned out, was also an accident.

In those frenzied days, news and rumours travelled incredibly fast and caused panic and violence in such a short space of time. Even for us expats living in the safe part of Khartoum, those few days were chaotic, crazy, tiring and disorientating. Over 130 people died. Our Sudanese friends and colleagues were reduced to tears when recounting how they had seen people stabbed, and another saw a little boy shot by the police. For a few hours Sudan stared down the barrel of open warfare once again. It would have been ugly and very bloody. It was suddenly easy to see how Rwanda, where the plane had been shot down, where the leaders and mass media had called for reprisals rather than peace, where the Government soldiers led the killings rather than prevented them, had happened. The Rwandan killings, with all the ingredients for a genocide in place, suddenly seemed a most natural and obvious process.

History proves that when under attack, leaders, including good and religious leaders, will call their people to arms. In Rwanda church leaders were known to turn into murderers. In the chaos of those few days in Khartoum, imams called for retaliation. Thankfully, in Khartoum, most of the key leaders kept their heads and appealed for calm.

I have no idea why God allowed that helicopter to crash and John Garang, a leader for the whole of Sudan, to die three weeks into office, where his stature was greatly missed in the subsequent months. However, somehow I came out of the week with more hope for Sudan than I ever had before. As we stared at a return to full scale war between north and south, I suddenly saw how far the country had moved on. Almost imperceptibly the peace had spread. I first worked in Sudan five years before; the outlook and prospects of peace then were desolate. I would never have believed Garang could have been sworn in as Vice President and that on his death his deputy would quickly be appointed to replace him. And so I can see now, more clearly, how God has moved this country on and I believe he will continue to do so. Peace will come to Sudan, I feel it more strongly than ever before.

The burial of Garang was in Juba in South Sudan. It was a city he had fought and failed to capture in twenty-two years of fighting, but she now welcomed him with open arms, hailing him her hero. Previously it was a city controlled by the Government. Now at Garang's funeral the former southern rebels stood next to their once loathed enemies – now their Muslim colleagues of Government – and were united in heartfelt mourning for a great fighter, leader and visionary. As John Garang's wife said, he may be dead but his vision of peace remains alive. It is our job, through prayer and action, to make that dream a reality.

The Lord is My Shepherd

During their morning devotion, the team in Beida read Psalm 23. 'The Lord is my shepherd... Even though I walk through the valley of the shadow of death, I will fear no evil, for you are with me; your rod and your staff, they comfort me.' It proved a prophetic passage, for unaware to them, in the next few hours they were due to see what 'valley of death' meant in the Darfur context.

The day before, Tearfund vehicles had had one shot fired over them on the road running parallel with the Sudan–Chad border, an area known for lawlessness and rebel activities. Our analysis was that they had deliberately shot over the vehicle to let us know they were there, but because they recognized Tearfund as an NGO doing good work for their people they had intended no harm. We had driven that road many times for the past year safely and we trusted in our 'acceptance' (once before a similar incident had occurred). Our analysis and trust was proved to be misplaced.

After finishing the devotions a convoy of seven vehicles (including vehicles from other NGOs) returned along that road. The vehicles were stopped by fifteen to twenty armed men who led the vehicles off the road and then dragged everyone out at gunpoint. Guns were held to heads, the men were put in a semicircle and badly beaten with whips and rifle butts; heads and backs were walked and stamped on. One of the women was dragged aside into the bushes and, with their male friends and colleagues within earshot, was hurt and abused. The remaining women, having been made to lie in the middle of the semicircle were then stripped and forced to endure a variety of beatings whilst pleading for their lives. Darren, the team leader, was told, whilst at gunpoint, to kneel, which meant he saw most of the ordeal. Later he was told to lie down. (As he was doing so he recalled the verse 'He makes me lie down in green pastures', which had been read that morning.)

Eventually the rebels stopped their physical assaults and, having made everyone suffer the baking sun for three hours, stole money, cameras, satellite phones and left. A while later Darren dared to look up from the ground. He saw next to him a Bible, opened it up and the first thing he read was 'The Lord is your strength'. He got up, quickly applied first aid to those bleeding the most, led the team back into the vehicles and drove off as fast as possible. Some of the staff were injured so badly they needed emergency assistance and were flown to Khartoum hospital. The response from other NGOs (Medair, MSF[3]) and the UN (OCHA[4] and DSS[5]) was very supportive.

While the degree of the physical injuries varied, all had been through a highly traumatic incident. Within forty-eight hours, Tearfund had a counsellor on the ground, flown in from London, to work with team members. To this day we do not know who was behind the attack, nor why.

Rachel and I were on a plane to join my family for a holiday in Spain. As we took off from Madrid to Malaga (the final leg of the journey), my phone went, but as we were about to take off, I could not take the call. I recognized the London number and in my heart of hearts knew something was wrong. We landed in Malaga having travelled for seventeen hours. My father and brother were waiting but I turned on my phone to listen to a voice message explaining the details of the above incident. Like everyone I was in a state of shock and spent much of that night on the phone to people in London, Khartoum and Darfur. Throughout the holiday I was regularly on the phone to my colleagues and friends in Sudan. The incident hung like a pall over my mind and meant I was emotionally distanced from my family as I struggled to process it in my head and prayers.

On the return flight, we had time in Cairo airport. I sat down and wrote the following to Darren, the team leader who reported to me. He was relatively new to Tearfund and had led the team through the whole incident and aftermath whilst struggling with his own shock. The letter was written as much for me as it was for him.

Dear Darren,

I'm writing this in Cairo airport. Its been a funny week for me. Like everyone I was shocked by the news, but felt very powerless in a situation where every natural instinct in you wants to try and help – like a mother separated from her suffering child. In the end I realized there was little I could do except pray, so every day Rachel and I (together and separately) tried to lift all of you up to the Lord in prayer and commit you into his arms.

Various thoughts and reflections came to me during the week and in my prayer times, so I thought I would share them with you. I've never been in or through a situation that you have and so I do not suggest I understand what it was like. Clearly you have stared evil in the face and that evil touches our spirit in a very profound way leaving us shocked and revolted.

I have no idea why God allowed you to experience such an incident. I never will! But in my lowest and most difficult moments and times in my life, one turns to Christ and realizes afresh that he can relate to everything one has been through. Not only was he with you in a spiritual sense, but also as a human he went through a similar and worse trial.

I read also about the death of John the Baptist who faithfully followed Jesus and it resulted in his head being decapitated and placed on a platter. Sometimes following Jesus is dangerous, sometimes it is painful. He never said it would be easy.

If you are feeling responsible for what happened to your staff, then Jesus probably felt the same. John suffered death after choosing to follow Jesus: sometimes

One of the underlying causes of the conflict in Darfur is desertification.

Since the conflict began, rape has been used as a weapon of war on the displaced population and many women are too scared to leave their camps.

Forced displacement. This community of 168 families were forced to move their village in order to escape frequent threats on their lives, assaults and theft. In total, over 2.5 million people have had to move home as a result of the conflict. In the background a UN helicopter, used because the roads are too dangerous, is arriving with supplies'.

Much of our work was with children. We set up clubs in order to teach them about health and help them overcome the trauma of war. Fifty-eight thousand children attended our clubs on a weekly basis across Darfur.

Children learning about mosquito nets.

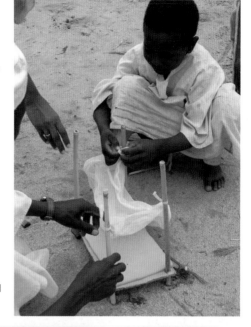

One of the grievances of the rebels is that they feel marginalized by the government. The shot below is of a dilapidated school, bereft of investment.

We would occasionally reflect on Jesus' words, 'I have come that you might have *life in abundance*' and aim to outwork them in our project. Above is a water point we rehabilitated. In total we reached over 70,000 people with water.

Garsilla airstrip in Darfur. Rachel is six months pregnant. Little was I to know that in a few weeks time I would return to this airstrip following the death of Rashid Mohammed Mohammed Adam (one of our drivers) in a nearby riot.

Bishop Hilary (above) and Reverend Enoch (right) holding Iona, our daughter, during a Tearfund conference. Both men have been an inspiration to me in the way that they maintained their faith through years of war, refuge, poverty and struggle, while leading and shepherding the church when peace seemed nothing more than a faint hope.

The worst Haboob (dust storm) experienced in Khartoum for twenty years. Dust filled the air and turned the day into night. These pictures show the storm rolling in over the Blue Nile.

as a leader your followers will suffer as well. Jesus must have been tempted by guilt, self-recrimination and wondering whether the cost was worth it. He must have felt the grief of his loved one who, after doing as Jesus told him, suffered and died in such a revolting way. Jesus understands how you are feeling, he has been through worse.

Many times I have prayed the prayer of Philippians 3:10: 'I want to know Christ and the power of his resurrection and the fellowship of sharing in his sufferings'. Somehow through your sufferings you can come to know Christ better and what he went through for you. And then in your healing 'somehow...attain the resurrection from the dead.'

Rachel and I read *The Purpose Driven Life* [a book I knew Darren had] and I quote from it:

It is...painful experiences...that God uses the most to prepare you for ministry. God never wastes a hurt! In fact, your greatest ministry will most likely come out of your hurt. Who could better minister to parents of a Down syndrome child than another couple who have a child afflicted in the same way?

...God intentionally allows you to go through painful experiences to equip you for ministry to others. The Bible says, 'He comforts us in all our troubles so that we can comfort others. When others are troubled, we will be able to give them the same comfort God has given us.'

If you really desire to be used by God, you must understand a powerful truth: The very experiences that you have resented or regretted most in life – the

ones you wanted to hide and forget – are the experiences God wants to use to help others. They are
your ministry!... People are always more encouraged when we share how God's grace helped us in
weakness'.[6]

> Jesus said to Peter: 'You do not realize now what I
> am doing, but later you will understand.'

After the death of John the Baptist, Jesus' response was
firstly to withdraw (take a holiday) but soon afterwards
he fed the 5,000. We need that Christ-like balance of
solitude and prayer but we are not to mope around forever...pressing on 'toward the goal to win the prize for
which God has called [us] heavenward'.[7]

Revelation 12 gives us a glimpse of the enormous
spiritual struggle which exists unseen by us. We are in
a spiritual battle. We are working in one of the darkest
corners of the earth – flying the banner of love, of
peace, of Christ. No wonder we are under attack of
every form. We often glibly use Paul's words, 'fight the
good fight'. But if we are serious about that we must be
prepared to be hurt. The bigger the fight; the greater
the pain.

In Mark 7, Jesus healed a girl of demons. After such
an event we will, I'm sure, all carry our own demons,
memories, fears, guilt, recrimination, and pain. Over
time I'm sure Jesus can and will free us from those
demons and heal us completely, if we consistently
come to him in faith.

Then I have been reading some of the psalms and
share these prayers:

'May your unfailing love come to me, O Lord'
(119:41)

'Though I walk in the midst of trouble, you preserve my life; you stretch out your hand against the anger of my foes, with your right hand you save me.'
(138:7)

Maybe some of this is helpful
God bless
Ed

For just as the sufferings of Christ flow over into our lives, so also through Christ our comfort overflows.
(2 Corinthians 1:5)

Newsletter Home

At Christmas 2005, Rachel and I sent home the following newsletter.

The last few months have been marked by a lot of insecurity, especially in the areas where we work in West Darfur, based out of Geneina.

On 1 August one of our vehicles was shot at and hit.

On 1 September, a convoy of our vehicles was stopped by an armed rebel group. Both these incidents were on the same stretch of road and we have not used the road since.

For two months after the above incident we barely

went back to the field and only then with the use of UN helicopters so we could avoid the road. During that time there were more than forty attacks on other NGOs in West Darfur.

In November, aided and advised by UN security, we began to slowly return to the communities and projects.

This is an account of my last week:

After work on Sunday, whilst the fighting was still going on in Masterei, I went to church. During the sermon I received a phone call. One of our guards had been shot. At the time we thought it was in the leg but it later turned out a bullet had entered his buttock and left his lower back.

I came back to my seat and prepared for communion, trying to work out how Christ's death related to the phone call I had just received. I took the wine.

'This is my blood'.

How does his blood, affect the situation of our guard, a poor Muslim, currently shedding his own blood in a thatched hut? What difference does it make?

'Given for you'

'Sorry God, I fail to see how that helps those wounded right now, or the people we are going to have to leave as we evacuate.'

'You could argue that were it not for church (i.e. Tearfund), we would not have been able to evacuate the guard to a hospital and safety.'

'I am grateful for the church you established...but that hardly seems to account for the countless others currently bleeding, and the dozens of questions firing through my head.'

I stood and tried to get through the final hymn, singing through my tears.

The guard and three of our Sudanese staff were evacuated to Geneina the next day. The guard is recovering, he and his family are very grateful for the help. Rachel and I flew into South Darfur to another project site on the same Monday.

On Tuesday, I was in a camp where we have a feeding centre. I saw a child I had first met in September. Since then he had been cured from malnutrition and discharged from the programme. Within a few weeks he had been readmitted with severe malnutrition. It is hardly surprising: his mother is mentally ill, they are living in a camp with virtually no NGOs there, their house is a hut the size of my bathroom, he has five siblings all under eight, his father was absent (working far away to try and earn money); their homes, fields, villages and schools were destroyed over fifteen months ago. This family was desperately poor, Tearfund are keeping their child alive.

I spoke to a few others in the camp: 'Will you return this dry season?' I asked hopefully. They were all adamant they would not. 'It is too dangerous to return, there are no schools and all our houses are destroyed.' Clearly this will be a protracted conflict. We will be here next year, in the same camps with the same people.

Still Tuesday – I received another call from the same team from Sunday: 'We have evacuated from Congo

Haraza to Beida and declared Beida level 4 [too dangerous to remain]. Armed militia have surrounded Congo Haraza and destroyed our water point. (Each water point will supply water to thousands living in a camp.) Mortar and rapid gunfire can be heard.'

Our team, with staff from other NGOs, lay low for the night, ready to drive off should the fighting come closer. The UN helicopters evacuated them the next morning.

This was the second evacuation in three days for the same team. We are grateful none of our staff were hurt, but deeply frustrated at our inability to help these people. When they really need our help, we have to leave. All the hours planning projects have to be put aside, and in deep disappointment we wait to see how the situation develops, evacuate all our non-essential staff from Geneina, wonder what the future may hold and hope that soon it will be safe enough to continue the work we are desperate to do.

I first came to Sudan over five years ago and have spent the majority of that time working in Sudan (or supporting the work from London). In that time I have seen huge progress in the south, which was unimaginable in 2000. Whilst I recognize the huge difficulties which lie ahead, the progress over five years gives me hope, strength and faith for the future of Sudan. As I look back I can see the almost imperceptible hand of God miraculously moving the country forward.

By contrast when I look at Darfur I find myself hugely upset at the enormous suffering; deeply angry at the selfish land-grabbing and murder which continues unabated and is affecting millions; frustrated by the insecurity which prevents us from working and people returning to their homes; struggling to see a solution in the face of such complex problems. I suppose the history of the south can give us faith and hope for the future of Darfur.

We miss you all very much and wish you every blessing for Christmas, a time when we are reminded that God is with us. He is with us in our doubts, fears, struggles and weaknesses. He is with us in Darfur.

Building Bridges

Whilst Sierra Leone has a large Muslim population, it could not be described as an 'Islamic State'. North Sudan and Darfur most definitely can and so moving to Khartoum was a new experience of working within a Muslim context. One of the thoughts that struck me early on was of the staggering failures of mankind to have developed lasting and mutually trusting relationships between 'Caucasian/Christian/Western peoples' and the 'Middle Eastern/Muslim/Arab populations'.

Plotting history from the time of the crusades, through the Ottomans to present day Iraq highlights a sad picture of recurring enmity. We Westerners, if we are honest, perhaps struggle with an image of Muslims as oppressive fundamentalists with poor respect for human rights and poor treatment of women. However, it is not difficult to see how the average Muslim, living in the Middle East, might equally see the West as oppressive, fundamentalist, with a poor respect for human rights. Through their eyes, the West has set out to free Iraq from a dictator that killed innocent civilians and tortured prisoners and replaced it with an army that has killed innocent civilians and tortures prisoners. Often their notions of Christianity are very wrapped up with their view of the Western culture and politics. Therefore from their perspective, the torture and the killing of innocents is associated with their understanding of the west...and by default Christianity.

Sudan suffers similar fault lines. The war with the south, in part, split the country between 'Arab/Muslim' and 'African/Animist/Christian'. Millions of southerners fled the war and live in the squatter camps in Khartoum. Therefore we employ both southerners and northerners, the former tend to join us for morning Christian prayers before work and the latter, with their prayer mats, take time out during the day to find a quiet spot for their own devotions. We occupy our own tiny world of Muslims and Christians working together, day-in, day-out. A small benefit of Tearfund operating in north Sudan therefore is the relationships we, as a distinctly Christian NGO, build with our Muslim colleagues. Below are four examples that touched me.

Following the death of John Garang in a helicopter accident, Khartoum city burst into violence. The riots split the city down the same ethnic/religious/political lines as the north-south war which had ended eight months before. Those few days drew the office closer together as southern Christians chaperoned northern Muslims home and vice versa. We regularly phoned each other up to ensure everyone was alright and assure one another of our prayers.

In May 2006 we decided to have a day of prayer and fasting for the insecurity in West Darfur which was preventing us getting out of the main town and into the field. Tearfund tapped into its network of prayer supporters, other Christian NGOs joined in and we received a number of heartening emails from people in England and Europe who joined us in prayer. We encouraged all our staff to join us as well. Muslims, of course, are no strangers to fasting or prayer and I think are sometimes pleased when they see Christians do a bit of it as well. In the morning staff meeting we explained a little about why we were praying, closed with a fairly awkward 'Christian' prayer and then went about our day's work. At lunch time, the Christians gathered, read the Bible and sang some fellowship songs while the Muslims took their prayer mats, lined up outside the front door and also prayed for peace in Darfur. I was moved by their devout, honest and heartfelt commitment and thanked Salafa the next day. She replied: 'Ed, this is our country and we are very moved when we see you praying and fasting for it. We must do the same. You have also encouraged us.'

I am not sure how one gets one's theological head around that, but I believe God answered our prayers: within a week we were back into the field and remained there for five months; compared to the previous nine months where we had barely spent a week in the field in one stint.

It was Rachel's last day in the office before she left for England and began her maternity leave. She was due to return to Khartoum but all the staff were keen to buy her a 'leaving present'. Salafa organized the whip-round and then went out and chose the gifts. Before the presentation, she gave me a preview. Tears welled in my eyes as I realized that Salafa, a committed Muslim, recognizing how important Christianity was to Rachel, had bought her a necklace and the soon-to-arrive baby a brooch, both of which carried a golden emblem of the cross.

In West Darfur, I remember sitting under a tree with some Muslim Darfurian colleagues on the edge of a large onion field which we had helped farmers cultivate. It is an important mandate of Tearfund's to work with people on all sides of the conflict, irrespective of race, creed or religion, and we were discussing how best to expand our projects to some different tribes. Some of the colleagues struggled with the concept of supporting people groups who they deemed adversaries and who came from tribes that had perpetrated the worst atrocities in the war. In trying to work through this issue we were able to discuss the words of Jesus – someone respected by Muslims – to 'love your enemy'. For guys who had suffered themselves, it was interesting to see them work through, grapple with and finally understand the logic behind those words and how we could apply them, in a practical sense, to their Darfur environment.

Riots and Killing in Darfur

The vehicles arrived in Deleige, a town half an hour north of our base in Darfur, at 10.00 a.m. About 11.00 a.m. a radio call came through from the driver, Rashid, that their vehicles had been surrounded by angry crowds. It turned out to be the last anyone heard from Rashid. For the next three or four hours the staff in Garsilla tried to piece together what was happening. It was too unsafe to go, and so they had to sit and wait as different rumours seeped through. Was one dead? Was it two? Was it staff from another NGO? Maybe they were all dead? Joseph Johnny, who runs the health education, immediately led a team of people into prayer.

During July 2006 there had been unrest in several camps: one week previously three Government staff had been killed in a camp 90 kilometres away. The killings followed false rumours that they were poisoning the water in the camps. The same rumours had reached Deliege. We were not sure whether to send the convoy, but were reassured that other NGOs were, and it was a camp in which we had brilliant relations. We had worked there for twenty months, over 5,000 children and 600 women had attended our health clubs (a project to teach children how to prevent disease and deal with their trauma) and we had helped hundreds of families restart their agriculture. We did not provide water in the camps and so we thought we were unlikely to be linked to these rumours.

Tragically, we were linked. As Tearfund staff approached the local school, children ran away, scared. This IDP camp, like dozens of others in Darfur, constituted 20,000 people living in 'open prisons': they had been terrorized, regularly beaten, raped and killed by their oppressors. Previously they had lived in dispersed settlements surrounded by their farms and cattle; for the past two years they had lived in the squalor of densely populated camps. It is not difficult, then, to understand how such conditions generate a bonfire ready to flare up: the firewood of suppressed anger, illiteracy and ignorance makes people vulnerable to paranoia. The rumours only doused that bonfire with fuel, and the children running away lit the match, which sparked the camp into flames.

The Tearfund local staff, Habeeb and Taha, were well known to the people in that camp. When people accused them of harming their children, they reasoned with them, reminding them of all Tearfund had done, emphasizing their common tribe and ancestry. Chiefs rallied to their cause and tried to calm the people down. However, as tensions began to rise, the numbers grew; the people soon turned into a crowd which in turn grew into a mob and later a riot. Taha and Habeeb grew increasingly anxious; when the women began to sing a war chant, they were terrified. On hearing the threats to burn them, Taha made a bolt for it, sprinting for the protection of the police station. The crowd caught him and beat him, stabbing him in the head and back, kicking and thumping him. They left him for dead. Thankfully their diagnosis was wrong and Taha was only pretending. The pretence saved his life.

As Taha bolted, Habeeb ran in a different direction and eventually hid in a hut; he tried to escape, dressed as a woman, but was recognized, fled again and finally hid in a latrine. Only a grass wall screened him from view as, for two hours, he listened to people baying for his blood. 'We have killed one, there is one more to go... We know he is here somewhere, if you find him, kill him,' they said. Habeeb, sat there, believing his friend Taha to be dead and fearing he would be next. After two hours he smeared himself in mud and walked towards the police, who eventually shielded him to safety.

We know the story of these two because they escaped; we know less about the driver Rashid. The doctor's report said he was stabbed to death, killed by six incisions to the skull. Two vehicles were also burned.

The hours between the radio call and the bodies (dead

and alive) being returned to Garsilla were tense for everyone at the base. It was almost impossible to separate fact from fiction. We in Khartoum were kept informed as things developed and for an hour or two there was that sinking dread of the unknown in the pit of the stomach. When confirmation of the news finally came through, a dark cloud descended over our minds and hearts. It was as though the magnet in my compass had lost its strength and my inner arrow didn't know which way to point.

Focusing was difficult, yet focus is exactly what we had to do – for immediately we were informing London, other field teams, the UN, and other staff. We were working out how to inform the family, what compensation we should give, and whether we should medi-vac Taha. The phone never stopped ringing, as people phoned to confirm the news or offer condolences and support.

David Bainbridge, the Senior Operations Manager in London, ever committed, flew out from London. The decision was made that I would fly with him to Garsilla. At the time Rachel was in England, less than three weeks from the due date of our first child. Had she gone into labour whilst I was there, I would have had to miss the birth due to the irregular flights to and from Garsilla.

The days we spent with the team were consoling to me and I believe to others in the base. The fact that David had come from London sent a strong message of support to everyone and showed that Tearfund cares deeply about its staff. We met the relatives of the deceased Rashid – a Muslim family who were handling it all with enormous dignity. Sitting with them in the fading light of early evening as Dave assured them of Tearfund's condolences and prayers from all over the world was a profound privilege.

We met Taha in hospital in Nyala and were able to listen to him as he recounted his side of the story. He (along with others) was convinced there was 'another power' spreading these rumours. His mother was with him and was able to comfort and pray for him as he suffered nightmares every night. We also had the privilege of praying for him, which he said was an encouragement. In Garsilla, we met Habeeb who explained in precise detail all that had occurred. He broke down in tears, unable to believe he had been so betrayed by his own people. Both Habeeb and Taha were convinced that God and the prayers of Joseph Johnny and the others had miraculously delivered them from death. They said they had felt guided by another presence. We also met Taha's wife: in the hours immediately following the incident, while she believed her husband to be dead, she suffered a miscarriage. I spoke with other staff: One said she could not rid the image of Rashid from her dreams, another said he awoke at 2.00 a.m. unable to sleep further. Others struggled to concentrate on the most straightforward tasks.

The week in the field reminded me again how all humans suffer the same symptoms of stress following such an incident. If this is how we struggle after one death, how much more traumatized must other Darfurians be in a war which has claimed an estimated 180,000 deaths? It reminded me how being with people and encouraging them is far more important work than email or attending meetings. It showed me how in times of suffering, Muslims and Christians alike, although we have different notions of God and Christ, all come to God for solace and in times of suffering we both turn to faith in prayer.

In the weeks following the incident the community felt too ashamed to contact Tearfund and so in mid September Habeeb took the first brave step in reconciliation. The people said they did not deserve to have Tearfund work for them again, yet Tearfund urged reconciliation.

Mike Barton, the Area Coordinator, wrote the following:

> They were a people who had done wrong, a people who felt they were undeserving of any mercy because of what they had done. In the midst of this despair here was an act of forgiveness and reconciliation; love being shown to people who felt they didn't deserve it; light shining in the darkness.

Notes

1. Much destruction continued to occur after June 2004. Most notably over 100,000 displaced arrived in Guereda around the end of 2005.
2. Genesis 4:2: 'Abel kept flocks, and Cain worked the soil'. Interestingly, after Abel had been killed, the Lord said: 'Your brother's blood cries out to me from the ground' (Genesis 4:10).
3. Médecins Sans Frontières.
4. Office for Coordination of Humanitarian Affairs.
5. Department for Safety and Security.
6. Rick Warren, *The Purpose Driven Life*, Zondervan, 2003, pages 246–7.
7. Philippians 3:14.

CHAPTER EIGHT

Killing: How Do We Respond?

At the time of writing the final draft of this book (April 2007), Rachel and I are still in Khartoum, working in Darfur, and have extended our placement for one more year. To end the book, I share some of my thoughts in answer to two questions that have continually challenged me during this work.

How Can a Man Kill Innocent Women or Rape Young Girls?

The depths of man's savagery can leave us horrified, sickened and shocked. One particularly gross example, that struck me early on, is described below; but I heard of many, many more and some instances of rape are too sick to put into print.

When back in England, I am often asked why there are so many wars in Africa. Sometimes it feels like the subliminal question (even if people don't always realise it) is whether there is something unique or different with Africans. I guess therefore one of the reasons for exploring this question is to show that in a given set of circumstances we all are capable of acts of extreme violence. Similar incidents have occurred on every continent, in every war, which suggests they are the result of a certain combination of stresses. It suggests that war has a power that pushes people to their most carnal extremes. Reading a few books on the psychology of killing and rape has helped me understand more fully how humans get to such a point. And understanding helps us forgive.

On my first assignment in Burundi, a matter of miles from our base in the north of the country an attack occurred on a camp for displaced people. The attackers, armed with machetes, hacked indiscriminately against anyone they could find, including women and children. I cannot remember exactly the number dead, but I believe it to be seventeen. Casualties were also carried to the hospital with large chunks hacked out of their heads, limbs and bodies.

Similar stories seem to have occurred in every war zone I have read about. I find it relatively easy to relate to how someone can dispassionately drop bombs on a target a few miles below, or even pull the trigger at a faceless human-shaped blob a few hundred metres away. But how someone can attack an innocent female and drive a blade into her is far more difficult to empathize with.

Before going out to Burundi, I read an article in a respectable newspaper, propagating the theory that humans in central Africa could achieve such staggering depths of savagery because they were lower down in the human evolutionary chain. I do not agree. Human beings are human beings. Incidents such as My Lai in Vietnam or even, to a lesser extent, Abu Ghraib in Iraq, suggest that such savagery is not an unfortunate side-effect of a war, but an unavoidable result, created by the negative energy of war. The combined mix of corruption, dehumanizing the enemy, the addiction and adrenaline of killing, peer pressure and the intoxicating power of evil might help explain why these events occur.

Corruption

The book *Captain Corelli's Mandolin* begins by painting a pre-war picture of an almost idyllic Greek Island setting. A late adolescent girl, Pelagia, is falling for a late adolescent lad, Mandras. Mandras is a lovable, charming, kind, young rogue. As the war breaks out he is conscripted and sent to fight the Italians invading Greece. During his time away he suffers hardships almost unimaginable: frostbite, hunger, terrible sanitation, and war at its most brutal. He left home utterly unprepared for war and returned scarred emotionally and physically. Neither endeared him to Pelagia and so their love affair ended. Distraught, Mandras left the island a lost soul. As a wayward layabout he was taken in by misguided communists who taught him how to read and poisoned his innocent mind with perverted beliefs and philosophies. They forced him to beat an old man. He was reluctant at first but then 'it became an exhilaration. It was as if every rage from the earliest year of childhood was welling up inside him, purging him, leaving him renewed and cleansed.'[1] Later he was forced to shoot the man in the head. Once innocent blood was on his hands, without reprisal, there was no turning back. He was a rapist and a killer. The author shows how easy it is, in a matter of months, for an innocent, likeable young lad to be turned into a savage killer.

How can someone kill another man? Innocent minds can easily be corrupted and twisted to evil ends. Chris Hedges, a war correspondent of fifteen years, writes: 'It takes little in wartime to turn ordinary men into killers. Most give themselves willingly to the seduction of unlimited power to destroy and all feel the heavy weight of peer pressure. Few, once in battle, can find the strength to resist.'[2]

An American soldier in Vietnam came to the same conclusion: 'You put those same [American] kids in the jungle for a while, get them real scared, deprive them of sleep and let a few incidents change some of their fears to hate. Give them a sergeant...add mob pressure, and those nice kids who accompany us today would rape like champions.'[3]

Dehumanizing the Victim

In Burundi, I heard of rebel leaders who forced their followers to eat human flesh. Sometimes they tricked them into it by placing man meat in the pot. They recognized that once you have eaten the flesh of another man, a line has been crossed and your respect for them declines. Children captured by the Lord's Resistance Army (a rebel army fighting in northern Uganda and southern Sudan), after being repeatedly raped, 'were forced to stab corpses. They were only allowed to stop when their captor decided he had seen enough blood spurting on to their clothes and bodies.'[4] In order to turn them into killers 'they have to be brutalized, their nascent sense of what is right and what is wrong erased...overcome by guilt and self-loathing, they subsequently shut out reason and emotion. In this numb state they do their master's bidding, however gruesome the task.'[5]

A question explored after the Second World War was how so many Germans could have killed so many Jews. It must be the same for all genocides. One of the explanations put forward was that the victims were dehumanized. The leaders managed to dehumanize their victims and, crucially, convince their followers to do so as well. The killers no longer related to the humanity of those they killed; they objectified them and reduced them to something far lower than themselves. Their victims had become stigmatized, despised, hated, blamed for all their ills and so were almost deserving of their punishment. Somehow the reality of these killers had become distorted, they had lost sight of truth. Of course by dehumanizing others they dehumanized themselves. A part of their humanity was lost and they too, therefore, become victims of the war and of their own crimes.

The Thrill and Addiction of Killing

In Sierra Leone we were infested by rats. My natural reaction to such a problem was to pretend they were not there. If I heard a scurrying sound, it might be something else. And if they were there, I was happy to let us cohabit in peaceful harmony. I could pretend they didn't exist and they could do whatever they liked.

My colleague Janet, with whom I was sharing the accommodation, didn't share my feelings. Janet's senses appeared to be honed in to the rats in a manner entirely opposite to mine: she turned that sixth sense, which so bemuses men, into a finely tuned rat-tracking device. I would stagger from my room bleary eyed in the morning, to see Janet staring behind some cupboard claiming: 'He's behind here, I know he is.'

Finally after Janet had awoken with rat poo on her pillow I had to agree she could no longer simply 'cohabit' with the furry foes. Rat traps were not working; a change in policy was needed for normal sanity levels to prevail.

I got my large shoes on and Janet, with courage only bestowed on bravehearted Scots, chased the rat into the open where I trembled with a large club. The first one came – I missed with the first shot but stamped hard with my left foot. My boot thudded down on the rat and it was no more! Success. With confidence high we followed the second rat into the office until it scurried out; one sharp jab to the head finished him off. The adrenaline pumped through our veins as we declared victory of man over rat. We felt a sense of relief, pride and joy because of our bravery, intelligence, and skill. Give me another rat – we could kill anything now. We were on a high. I realized later they were the first mammals I had ever killed.

After the war in Sierra Leone, child soldiers confessed their stories: They told of how initially they resisted harming anyone, but then, under enormous pressure, they committed their first kill. Soon it was a handful, and later they became both immune to their wrongs and almost attached to the power that killing brought. 'And they are, for a moment, gods, swatting down powerless human beings like flies.'[6] The adrenaline and high and power they received from killing became almost addictive. As a result they became detached from themselves and almost disintegrated as the cycle of evil took greater control of their lives, overcoming their humanity.

This high is not unique just to those in Sierra Leone. Lt. Col. Dave Grossman studied the psychology of killing (mainly in Vietnam) and concluded: 'Immediately after the kill the soldier goes through a period of euphoria and elation.' Grossman quotes a soldier from the First World

War, who after killing a Turk, wrote, 'I had a feeling of the most intense satisfaction.'[7] He also quotes others who compare the thrill and seduction of killing to that of sex. Once the natural resistance to killing is overcome, men find there is something in the act of killing which has an addictive power.

Peer Pressure

As well as the thrill and addiction to killing, the power of peer pressure is significant, especially when mixed with the recipe of extreme, intense or vulnerable situations. An experience I had in Burundi taught me how vulnerable I was to such pressure.

There was a military curfew at 10.00 p.m. across the city of Bujumbura, which meant we had to be home by 9.30. It was 9.15, and we were heading for our car and saw above us what looked liked shooting stars or fireworks. The sight was accompanied by the sound of popping which reinforced still further the association with fireworks. An instant later the penny dropped, and we ran inside. The sight was tracer bullets,[8] the sound was the crack of a gun. The first sounds were followed by many more. The crack of the gun was joined by the cackle of a machine gun and then the boom of mortar fire. We agreed to stay the night at Stefan's.

Stefan was a large, loud man of South African and Belgian extraction living in Burundi. He was the son of a colonel. He was rich, in his mid-thirties, with a strong character and powerful presence. Myself and Paula (also working for Tearfund) were to spend the night at his house with a few of his other friends. The sound of guns intensified and at times seemed very near. His house was not 50 yards from the president's palace and it was conceivable this was under attack. It was the first time I had heard a battle like this and it was unsettling. Stefan had heard it many times before and seemed to revel in it. It excited him – he disappeared into a room and marched out with his AK-47. He handed a pistol to one of his friends and came to me, as the only other male, with another cased pistol. 'You might need it' he said with certainty and assurance. I stared at the silver pistol. I was now completely unsettled. I had no idea how to react or what to do. I fingered the gun. Was I to carry it? What was I to do in this situation? It was a scenario I had never been in before, nor imagined I ever would be. I was lost and overloaded and did not know how to react. After a while the shaken kaleidoscope that was my mind returned to order and I could see once again. I replaced the gun in its box and timidly said, 'No thanks'. We watched a video and eventually went to bed.

My point is this. Here I was, a man in my early twenties, fully convicted of my principles, a Christian all my life, educated to degree level from a British university, someone with more than average self-confidence and self-esteem, and yet for a while I did not know what to do. It is perfectly obvious to me now that I should never have touched the gun, but at the time it wasn't. Imagine if the scenario had been even more intensified and I had been even more vulnerable: imagine if the shooting had been even nearer. Maybe also if there had been no women in the room, the peer pressure on me would have been greater. What if there were more men, all of them wielding guns and imploring me to as well? Would I have said no then? It is not inconceivable that I would have bowed to the peer pressure.

If that is true for me, imagine a child in Burundi, growing up with no mother or father. Maybe he has seen some of his relatives killed, maybe not. Certainly he could not have escaped the true stories of death which must haunt every village. Living as a peasant he is regularly hungry. With no education he is bored and illiterate. He joins a bunch of older lads, he lives in the forest, he is brainwashed with tribal hatred. His mind is poisoned, twisted and perverted. All the causes of his sufferings, he is told, are due to the other tribe.

He is shown a gun and taught how to use it. Killing chickens, goats, sheep, cows, monkeys, and wild animals is part of his everyday survival. Humans are only the next step up. Soon he may be forced to eat human flesh, then his respect for the human is so low that killing one is relatively easy. Somehow war fills a spiritual void within him. For redundant adolescents in a deprived area, be they bored Arab nomads in Darfur or impoverished, disaffected youths in Central Africa, Sierra Leone or Liberia, war gives them something to believe in, something to get up for, something into which they can channel their anger and energy. War is a force that gives them a meaning.[9]

As an aside, I think that war also gives meaning to the many reporters, UN workers and relief workers that work in them, sometimes in a healthy way, other times not. On a personal level I prefer who I am when I am overseas. My concerns – human suffering, poverty, and injustice – are much more worthwhile than when I am in England, where other issues – money, the football premiership, reality TV shows, and traffic jams – clamour so loudly for my attention.

In Sierra Leone, children were given drugs and forced into the front line. The drugs made them fearless fighters, those that survived had tasted the adrenaline of battle and the power in killing. Having killed your first victim, a psychological threshold is breached and your next is that much easier; turning back that much harder. The soldier is speeding along a slippery slope to becoming a serial, savage murderer. Soon this child is very capable of clubbing someone to death or cutting them up with a machete.

The Intoxicating Power of Evil

Finally there appears to be something in killing and war that grips people with an evil power. Even secular writers notice this: '[In the Second World War] mass murder and execution can be sources of mass empowerment. It is as if a pact with the devil has been made and a host of evil demons [are released]...empowering its nation with an evil strength as a reward for its blood sacrifices. Each killing affirmed and validated in blood the demon of Nazi racial superiority.'[10]

'Killing unleashes within us dark undercurrents that see us desecrate and whip ourselves into greater orgies of destruction.'[11]

If secular writers recognize it, then how much more so should we as Christians understand some of the spiritual powers at play behind a 'Rwanda Genocide' or other massacres?

Rape is harder for me to understand as nothing in me can relate to it, but I think all the above driving forces come together. (For example rape most often occurs in gangs where peer pressure is a factor.) The above factors break down long-established prohibitions against violence and at the same time, in a similar way, some of our sexual prohibitions too. This is why one often sees the crumbling of sexual and social norms as the domination and brutality of the battlefield is carried over into personal life. 'Rape, mutilation, abuse and theft are the natural outcomes of a world in which force rules, in which human beings are objects.'[12] 'The linkage between sex and killing becomes unpleasantly apparent when we enter the realm of warfare.'[13] When 'life becomes worth nothing, when one is not sure of survival, when a society is ruled by fear, there often seems only death or fleeting, carnal pleasure.'[14] There is something in war that inverts all moral order and hierarchies. The moral universe is turned upside down. In a functioning society criminals are put in jail, in a dysfunctional one (war), these criminals are often the ones who rise to the top.[15]

It is said that 2 per cent of a population have a tendency for psychopathic behaviour. War provides an environment for these behaviours to be expressed. When these guys are wielding power, people follow them. Only the very exceptional seem to have the moral courage to resist. And in such an environment, sex becomes less about lovemaking and more about exercising power and gratifying base instincts.

So perhaps understanding these interrelated factors of corruption, dehumanizing the victim, peer pressure, the addiction of killing and the power of evil, our emotions can soften from ones of anger and disbelief to ones of understanding and maybe even of pity. There but for the grace of God, have I gone.

From this point one can build upwards and begin to understand how clans, tribes and countries have risen against another. How the pressure to hate can be so great it can in part build towards a genocide. Many of the African armies and rebel movements begin with good ideologies, but lack the discipline and organization of Western armies and so are more susceptible to the lure of indiscriminate killing and rape. Genocide and widespread massacre perhaps is a harder leap of understanding and beyond the realm of this chapter.[16]

So where does that leaves us as Christians? How should we respond? Whatever one's view, what is certain is that it is a terrible tragedy that a child or young man can grow up learning to kill. The sad eyes of a child soldier reveal someone who has exchanged the joys and freedom of childhood, of games, education, and parental love for loss, hatred and trauma. Maybe those who forced them into it were themselves victims of the same abuse. Should we treat them as people in need, captives that need freeing, or should we see them as delinquents that require justice? Should we consign them to live on in their hell of existence and expect a divine vengeance? Are they victims or killers, or are they both? Maybe we are all to blame – maybe none of us are. Alexander Solzhenitsyn grappled with this question when he wrote: 'If only there were evil people somewhere insidiously committing evil deeds and it were necessary only to separate them from the rest of us and destroy them. But the line dividing good and evil cuts through the heart of every human being.'

I have heard of rulers, rebels and despots who have

established 'training camps' for children. Perhaps those who set them up with cold-hearted calculation, driven by a lust for power, should carry the greatest responsibility? 'Woe to those who *make* unjust laws.'[17] I met one man who had interviewed a number of such idealogues. He said on one occasion he had to end the interview early as he felt physically sick and reviled by the man. Maybe we can hold onto the fact Jesus also felt a similar distress and hinted at a hope of justice: 'But if anyone causes one of these little ones who believe in me to sin, it would be better for him to have a large millstone hung around his neck and to be drowned in the depths of the sea...*woe to the man through whom [the things that cause people to sin] come!*'[18] As a Christian who believes in the God of love, the subject of hell is not my favourite topic, and it is one I instinctively shy away from. It is, however, one referred to by Jesus, and by Paul: 'For since the creation of the world God's invisible qualities – his eternal power and divine nature – have been clearly seen, being understood from what has been made, so that men are without excuse.'[19] When staring at the darkest evils of perverting children, the fact that we will all have to give account might be a comfort. Though still I do not know who should receive this justice. I am not sure who should shoulder the blame for the tragedy of humans being turned into killers. If 'the requirements of this law are written on their hearts, their consciences also bearing witness'[20] then maybe we are all responsible for our actions.

I do not know. Certainly we can all repent from the sin in our own hearts and try to encourage others along a similar journey. None of us know what will happen when we die, but whilst living, we can encourage others towards repenting of the darkness that holds them back from the freedom of love.

No one is beyond hope or redemption. Nelson Mandela's watertight logic is full of understanding, grace, forgiveness and hope: 'No child is born hating another man because of the colour of his skin, or his background, or his religion. People must learn to hate, and if they can learn to hate they can be taught to love, for love comes more naturally to the human heart than its opposite. Even in the grimmest times in prison, when my comrades and I were pushed to our limits, I would see a glimmer of humanity in one of the guards, perhaps just for a second, but it was enough to reassure me and keep me going. Man's goodness is a flame that can be hidden but never extinguished.'[21]

All we can do is trust in God's forgiveness, grace, understanding and love and encourage others around us on a similar path. We cannot condemn anyone to being irredeemable, as Jesus reminded us on the cross, where a thief crucified alongside Jesus repented, and was promised paradise. God, it appears, is predominantly a God of grace who likes to transform some of the most hopeless cases, such as Saul, from killer to saviour. Our task then, like Jesus, is to associate with the 'scum' of society and trust, somehow, in his transforming power.

Notes

1.   Louis De Bernières, *Captain Corelli's Mandolin*, Vintage, 1995.
2.   Chris Hedges, *War Is A Force that Gives Us Meaning*, Anchor, 2003, page 87.
3.   American soldier quoted in Lt. Col. Dave Grossman, *On Killing*, Little, Brown and Co., 1998, page 191.
4.   George Alagiah, *A Passage to Africa*, Time Warner, 2002.

5.   George Alagiah, *A Passage to Africa*, Time Warner, 2002.

6.   Chris Hedges, *War Is A Force that Gives Us Meaning*, Anchor, 2003, page 171.

7.   Lt. Col. Dave Grossman, *On Killing*, Little, Brown and Co., 1998, page 111.

8.   Tracer bullets are bullets which light up their path and so show the shooter or an advanced sniper how near they are to hitting their target.

9.   In a parallel way war also gives meaning to others involved in the war. Experienced war reporters and even aid workers admit to being attracted to the thrill of war.

10. Lt. Col. Dave Grossman, *On Killing*, Little, Brown and Co., 1998, pages 208–9.

11. Chris Hedges, *War Is A Force that Gives Us Meaning*, Anchor, 2003, page 89.

12. Chris Hedges, *War Is A Force that Gives Us Meaning*, Anchor, 2003, page 104.

13. Lt. Col. Dave Grossman, *On Killing*, Little, Brown and Co., 1998, page 136.

14. Chris Hedges, *War Is A Force that Gives Us Meaning*, Anchor, 2003, page 168.

15. By way of an example, when the Darfur crisis broke, Musa Hilal was released from jail by the Sudanese Government and given orders to repress the rebellion.

16. George Alagiah's view is helpful: 'So many civil wars and conflicts... could be solved if the states concerned could deliver anything like the kind of life we in Europe take for granted. People who have the opportunity to make a living and to pass on the benefits to their children are unlikely to be seduced by the blandishments of class warriors or the peddlers of ethnic solutions to economic inequality.'

17. Isaiah 10:1, emphasis mine.

18. Matthew 18:6,7, emphasis mine.

19. Romans 1:20

20. Romans 2:15

21. Nelson Mandela, *A Long Walk to Freedom*, Abacus, 1995.

CHAPTER NINE

Suffering: Another Look

It was mid October 2000. I was sitting inside a mud and cement hut, losing once more at chess to Bashaw, my Ethiopian colleague. Night comes early in Sudan and 9.30 was very close to bedtime. There was a knock on the door and a voice asking for help. I did not react favourably to yet another request, and my instant thoughts were not enthusiastic. 'Please shut up, I am trying to play chess. Why did the guards let this man through? Can't it wait until tomorrow?'

It soon became clear this man could not wait until tomorrow. He had tried other NGOs, including the one he worked for, and they had all sent him away. Bashaw and I got into the vehicle and drove him to the set of huts that made up his compound. There were a number of relatives gathered around a woman in labour. Together we carried her into the pick-up, and drove through the town to the nearest thing to a hospital. Apparently there was one expat there, a Kenyan, who could operate. As we drove along, I tried to recall anything from my first aid training which might be of some help.

We got to the tented hospital and carried the woman into a ward full of other men and women. Many were naked, one had been shot. The blood from the woman dripped on to my foot, it had covered the back of the pick-up and was now staining the bed. Her child, now a few hours old, was carried in as well.

Whilst someone rushed off to find and rouse the doctor the rest of us did the best we could to nurse this woman. She looked at least 40, haggard and well worn. I was certain this would not have been her first birth and that her ageing breasts had fed many a child. She was in constant agony, writhing in pain. The bleeding continued.

I had no understanding of how bad the situation was. I had been in the country a short time, and had no background in medicine. But a few days earlier Martin, one of our staff, had lost his wife in childbirth, and it didn't take five years of medical training for me to realize this was quite serious. I kept wiping her sweat-ridden brow and tried to encourage the others, who were still looking to the white man for advice. Little did they know I was the least able in the room.

Under my breath I was praying hard and reaching out in faith for God to heal her. I knew it was within his power to do so. I reminded God that he had raised people from the dead. I claimed his promise that with sufficient faith we could move mountains. I informed God that I had absolute faith in him and that he therefore by rights had to heal this woman. 'Come on Lord, you can do it!'

There was no let-up in the pain or the bleeding of the woman. Never mind. I kept praying, I knew about persistent prayer. I knew Elijah had prayed for a long time before the child was raised. If God was testing me to see if I would persist in the prayer then no problem. I would pass the test.

It felt a long time before the doctor arrived. This was understandable, it was now past 11:00, he too got disturbed a lot, he too needed his rest.

It also seemed to take a long time to get the operating

theatre – also in a tent – ready. Eventually it was prepared, we moved the mother the 40 yards to the new tent, still she dripped a constant and visible trail of blood. Still I prayed.

It was evident to the doctor straight away that the patient would need blood and lots of it. The blood test takes ten minutes. That's fine, I said to myself. I know my blood group – O+ – and I am more than happy to donate. What a privilege that would be – for my blood to be used directly to save a life. What an answer to prayer.

There was little else I could do now but wait. The doctor was here, he knew what he was doing. So I left the naked body to his capable hands, took myself off and sat under a tree. I looked up into the sky. The nearest big city from Rumbek must be at least 1,000 kilometres away. There were no clouds and the stars looked magnificent. I looked at them and considered the hands which had made them. 'How simple, Lord, for you to heal this woman. You have made all the stars, what is this woman to you. You love her, I know you do. Reach out your hand now and touch her, perform a miracle.' I tried to continue praying in such a way. I hoped the spirit was interceding for me and leading my prayers.

After ten minutes I got up and returned to the foray.

'What's the news? What is her blood group? Tell the doctor I am O+.'

She was dead.

'This type of thing should never happen,' said the doctor. 'A very simple and common problem but it was just too long before they sought assistance from a qualified doctor. If this had happened in Nairobi there would have been an enquiry.'

We loaded the corpse, now clothed, back into the pick-up and drove the long drive back. Not a word was said. What could be said? Words fail us in moments such as these. It was now well after midnight, we unloaded the dead corpse and then in the next instance turned to see the tiny child being carried by a relative. Life and death so closely entwined. This woman had given her life that this child might live. There is no greater love.

Over the next week, I continued to try to visit the family. I tried to ensure the child got milk and I tried to pray for the life of that child. I knew how fragile life was in this part of the world – most of all for a newly born babe with no mother to feed and nurse it. A week or so before, Martin had lost his wife in a similar fashion. His child died a week later. I was determined this would not happen again.

The next Sunday, sitting under another tree, whilst listening to the church sermon in Dinka, I planned how I would spend my afternoon. Top of my list, ahead of writing letters and reading a book, was to visit the family and see how the child was. I forgot.

Next day, mid afternoon, as I was tapping away at something important on the computer, the radio operator came to the door with a message. I opened and read the note. The child had died the previous afternoon of diarrhoea.

So why is there so much suffering in the world? Why does God not answer our prayers? Why does he appear to stay silent?

Of all the questions Christians are faced with, these are the most difficult. Which of us, if we are honest, has never asked it and wondered or doubted in the goodness, power or existence of God? The question comes in many forms: how could God allow a flood to wipe out whole communities? Why has my boyfriend cheated on me? How could God allow bad to happen to me when I have been so faithful to him?

Having worked for an organization mandated to relieve death and suffering, it has at times felt as though my job is to stare pain in the face. I can't help constantly returning to this question, thinking about it, sniffing around it, trying to understand it... I probably always will. I have found no easy answers and probably never will. Perhaps the reason for me writing this is once again to try to find an answer.

At times I find trusting that God is actually good extremely hard. I have stood in church singing a worship song which proclaims that God is good. I stand there gritting my teeth, images of suffering flash through my mind, tears well up in my eyes and it takes every ounce of faith for me even to mouth the words 'Yes, the Lord is good'.

I have been a Christian all my life, grown up through church and read many Christian books. I know the 'textbook' answer to this question, I have heard it many times. And yet as I read the Bible I find that God seems to have precious little to say on the subject. In fact, it is almost as though God ignores the question altogether. I can't believe the question of suffering has not been asked by every generation including those around at the time of writing the Bible. So why is so little apparently said on the subject?

The Textbook Answer

The explanation for suffering I have heard most often runs something like this: God made a good earth and humans to dwell in it. God wanted and still does want the perfect, intimate relationship with humans. God made humans as incredible beings, highly intelligent and very capable. Our achievements are staggering – a man on the moon, the internet, genetic engineering, penicillin – all testifying to our abilities. God gave us all those gifts; he also gave each individual the gift of free will – the will to choose him or reject him. He had to do that to fulfil his desire for an intimate relationship: if he had made us without a free will we would have been robots, the relationship forced and contrived and therefore not perfect. Unfortunately the consequence of that free will is that, starting with Adam and Eve, we have all rejected him and by our sin made the world imperfect with illness and suffering. Following the resurrection of Christ, God is setting about redeeming the world and will restore all things to paradise at the time of the second coming.

This explanation is helpful – but also feels somehow inadequate when someone asks me how God could allow his entire family to be macheted to death. How he could allow 30,000 people to die in an earthquake. Why he ordains some to be born trapped by poverty and gives others the freedom of wealth and education.

A potential danger of learning such answers is that consciously or unconsciously one takes this answer verbatim as a cure for all ills and potentially forgets to face the problem. Some Christians are in danger of sweeping the difficulties in their life, or the suffering they see, under the carpet. They see suffering, they experience hardship and then they throw the textbook answer at the problem. The trouble is, rather than making the problem go away, it serves only to repress it.

As a Christian there is a lot of pressure to always appear happy. 'Do not worry – Jesus loves you.' It is almost as though it is a sin to be unhappy, after all, our peace should transcend all understanding.[1] Blind and forced happiness is unhealthy and wrong. As Christians we will suffer. If we never suffer as a Christian we are probably not following the teachings of Christ. How can we count the cost, carry the cross, hate our mother, father, wife, brother, sister and child, be persecuted, have compassion for the poor, or cry over lost souls if we do not suffer?

The psalms seem far more down to earth and in touch with humanity than some contemporary evangelists or writers. 'I pour out my complaint before [the Lord]';[2] 'My God, my God, why have you forsaken me?'[3] Even Jesus famously quoted this psalm when in agony on the cross. Many times David starts his psalms speaking out of his suffering, asking questions of God. His psalms are often angry. Then as the psalm goes on and he has spent time thinking about it and waiting on the Lord, he ends, 'and yet I will trust in the Lord,' or 'I will tell of all he has done'. Maybe for some of us this period of waiting will take weeks or even months before we can honestly say 'Yes, the Lord is good'.

Perhaps then, it is better to be honest with each other and with God and tell him we are suffering and struggling. John the Baptist, when in prison, doubted Jesus (Luke 7). John the Baptist had baptized Jesus, seen a dove come down from heaven and heard a voice from heaven say 'This is my son, whom I love'. Even with all this, John still questioned Jesus. He did not repress his doubts but sent his disciples to Jesus to find out the answer: 'Are you the one, or are we to expect someone else?' So, we too, when we have problems and when we suffer, must turn to God in an honest way, asking direct and difficult questions. Then Jesus will answer and our faith will be strengthened.

R.T. Kendal wrote, 'Repression is almost always a bad thing to do, but we often do it involuntarily because the pain seems too great to take on board. And yet we don't really get rid of the pain: we push it into the "cellar" of our subconscious, but it comes out in the "loft" of our lives...'[4]

There are a few examples where God is asked why there is suffering in the world:

1: Judges 6

The Israelites are being ravaged by the Midianites. As a result they are impoverished. An angel appears to Gideon and Gideon asks him a very direct question: 'If the Lord is with us, why has all this happened to us? Where are all his wonders...? ...But now the Lord has abandoned us and put us into the hand of Midian.' I love that question. The angel of the Lord has appeared to Gideon and instead of just accepting what the angel says, he speaks honestly, openly and very directly to the angel to the point of being rude. Basically, he asks, 'Why has the Lord allowed us to suffer? Surely God has abandoned us?'

God's reply makes me laugh – he never answers his question. He never tells Gideon why he has allowed all this to happen. It is almost as if he completely ignores the question. Rather he says 'Am I not sending you?...I will be with you.'

This is all we need to know. The Lord is sending us into

the world. The Lord will be with us. Gideon went out, the Lord was with him, miraculously he defeated the Midianites and people were saved from the yoke of oppression which caused their suffering.

Phillip Yancey tells a similar story – that of Martin Luther King.[5] At the start of his civil rights movement Martin, who had very recently become a father, received a phone call threatening his life and that of his child. He sat that night and prayed to the Lord asking if he should end the work he had barely started. Many questions must have been buzzing around his head...why should he have to be persecuted, was this sacrifice worth it, could he put his wife and child through this suffering? As he was praying, the Lord appeared to him in a vision and said only a few words: 'I will be with you' (the same words he said to Gideon). These words gave him the resolve to continue his work. Two days later a bomb exploded in his house. Neither Martin, nor his wife, nor his child was even injured. It was those words which continued to sustain Martin many a time through his life, as he was beaten, imprisoned, stabbed, mocked and scorned. For some reason God never explained to him why he must suffer; he never told him the good he would achieve, he simply told him that he would be with him. This is all he needed to say, it was all Martin Luther King needed to know, it was sufficient for him, it sustained and strengthened him.

It is interesting that the command repeated most often in the Bible is 'do not fear'. It occurs 365 times – once for every day of the year. Why is there suffering in the world? 'Do not fear. I have it under control.'

For some reason we may never know why we suffer. We may never know why some die of starvation whilst others are born into a wealthy existence. We will never understand why God made man capable of causing such evil. But God says to us, 'I am with you. Do not fear.' This then must be all we need to know, frustrating as it might be. I would love God to give me an answer to those questions, but he doesn't. His answer is 'I am with you.' This is sufficient for us, this will sustain us, this will strengthen us. And as we look back on those times in our life when we have suffered, we can testify to this truth. Yes, God was there. I may not have been aware of it at the time, but now I see he was there, holding me, carrying me, sheltering me, comforting me, leading me on. Had it not been for him my foot would have slipped. At times he was all I had...he was all I needed.

Also, as Jesus was suffering in Gethsemane, almost to the point of death, God sent an angel to strengthen him.[6] He didn't take away the cup, but helped him in the suffering. So too with us. God may not answer our direct requests, he may not take the suffering away, but if we pray to him he will help us in our suffering, he will send an angel in whatever form that takes, to help us. Even, I am sure, with the relatively small battles, God can send an angel to strengthen us.

2: Job

This is another story of suffering. The devil came to God and asked if he could allow Job – a righteous, holy and God-fearing man – to suffer. For some reason God accepted. He allowed Job to suffer. There follow thirty chapters of Job's suffering. Certainly he endured more hardship than most of us would ever bear in five lifetimes. He lost his family, his wealth, his friends, his health and his good name. Many times he calls out to God, often very directly: 'I desire to speak to the Almighty and to argue my case with God.'[7]

For some reason God appears to remain silent through many months of deep torment. Why does God do this? Why does he say nothing? Why did God grant the devil permission in the first place? Why did God not show his power, heal Job, miraculously return all his cattle and bring to life all his children? For some reason God chose not to do this. He chose instead, for a long period, to remain silent, distant and aloof.

Even when finally God does choose to speak he never answers the key question. He never tells Job why he suffered. Never. He pointedly avoids the questions altogether. Instead, in chapter 38, he points to creation. He mentions the birds, the rain, the snow, the stars, the clouds, the lions, the lightning. He directs Job's thoughts to the power of God. Effectively he says 'I am almighty...who are you to even ask me questions? Brace yourself like a man; I will question you and you shall answer me.'

There then follows some of the greatest prose ever written:

Where were you when I laid the earth's foundation?
Tell me, if you understand.
Who marked off its dimensions? Surely you know!
Who stretched a measuring line across it?

(Job 38:4,5)

God finally ends this monologue in chapter 40 with the words 'Will the one who contends with the Almighty correct him? Let him who accuses God answer him!'

Job's response appears fairly spot on: 'I am unworthy – how can I reply to you? I put my hand over my mouth.' But then God goes off on one again. Again he lectures Job: 'Would you discredit my justice?' And then finally it ends in chapter 42 with Job saying, 'Surely I spoke of things I did not understand'.

It is good to remember that we must fear God, that he is the almighty, the one who created the heavens and the earth. And who are we in relation to that? Can we even begin to question God?

Seldom do I keep this perspective to the suffering I see around me. In answer to God's question: 'Would you discredit my justice?' my most honest answer is yes! Lord, many times I stare at the world and I discredit it. I do not understand why women should have to be raped, why children should be abused, why man should be given such power they can destroy buildings, towns and cities in one blow. I do not understand why you allow innocent children to be hacked to death...and there I go again – talking 'of things I did not understand, things too wonderful for me to know'.[8] 'I am unworthy – how can I reply to you? I spoke once, but I have no answer – twice, but I will say no more.'[9]

Understand suffering? Don't even bother trying. If God does not feel us worthy to tell the answers, why should we consider it worth asking? This concept is above our human minds to grasp. He asks us to consider instead his great works and trust in him. This then is faith which comes from realizing who God is and who we are in relation to him. When we ponder God, his might and his creation, as the hymn writer articulates, we will end in praising God and our souls will sing for joy.

Oh Lord my God, when I, in awesome wonder,
consider all the works thy hand has made,
I see the stars, I hear the rolling thunder,
thy pow'r throughout the universe displayed.

Then sings my soul, my Saviour God, to thee:
How great thou art, how great thou art.[10]

3: Jesus' Response

One hears some sick stories of suffering. In Burundi, a soldier was attacked by rebels. He was decapitated, his penis chopped off, stuck in his mouth and his head then sent rolling down the hill to be found by his comrades. In Rwanda, rapists choose girls no older than two or three as they are less likely to be HIV positive. In Sudan a colleague confessed he had held a gun and watched as a fellow tribesman threw a baby of a different tribe into a burning hut. In Sierra Leone, two-month-old children have had their arms amputated. In Darfur a women was gang raped in front of her brother, then her genitalia were mutilated and thrown into her brother's face. In case you think this would never happen in Europe, in Croatia a man had his throat slit from one ear to another with a Black and Decker tool. Thousands were thrown into mass graves. In Germany nearly 6 million Jews were slaughtered. In Northern Ireland there are people who specialize in smashing kneecaps with a sledgehammer. In London a friend of mine, working in a hospital, told me of an eighty-year-old patient raped in her toilet cubicle.

Whichever way you look at it, there is no doubt that people from every culture and race are made capable of extreme and terrible evil. Is the God who created these humans really a good God?

Jesus was faced with exactly the same question. How many of us would dare choose his reply? Luke 13:1–3 reads: 'Now there were some present at that time who told Jesus about the Galileans whose blood Pilate had mixed with their sacrifices. Jesus answered, "…But unless you repent, you too will all perish."'

Again Jesus refuses to answer the direct question. He simply turns the tables back on us and says, 'Don't bother yourself with such questions…simply make sure you do not suffer a similar fate. Repent of your own sins, make sure you have your house in order…do not worry about the others. That is God's department, vengeance is his.'

Imagine someone asking the average postmodern-era Christian (such as myself) how God could allow the World Trade Center to collapse, killing more than 2,000 people. I think I would probably bumble some incoherent reply. Maybe a Biblical answer would go something like this: 'We don't always know the answers to these questions, but we do know that if we do not sort ourselves out with God then we too will face a similar fate.'

In Luke 13:4–5 Jesus said: 'Those eighteen who died when the tower in Siloam fell on them – do you think they were more guilty than all the others living in Jerusalem? I tell you, no! But unless you repent, you too will all perish.'

Jesus' Life and Suffering

R.T. Kendall writes: 'Jesus did not come into the world to explain suffering, he came into the world to save us from it.'[11] This argument seems to hold water. A blind man comes to Jesus and never does Jesus offer an explanation of why God allowed him to suffer all those years, he just heals him. When the paralytic is lowered to Jesus, Jesus doesn't appear too concerned about why God allowed him to suffer in that way. He is concerned firstly with his sin, which he saves him from by forgiving him, and then secondly he is concerned with his paralysis which he saves him from by healing him. Spiritual and physical healing – these seem to be the things Jesus was concerned with on earth. We Christians can sit down and pontificate about suffering all we like (as I am doing) but what good will it do? Jesus is concerned about saving us – in a very real way now with our daily problems, and in a much deeper and spiritual way by healing us of our sins which paralyse us. If these are Jesus' concerns they should be ours.

The other thing we can draw from Jesus' life is that he did know about suffering. Very few sufferings can we say Jesus did not experience. I have met people who have suffered enormous amounts: people living in refuge, people who have fled their homes in fear, lived through genocides, watched their family hacked to death, struggled with absolute poverty. Often I doubt that Jesus has suffered like some of these people, but Jesus lived through a genocide, he was a refugee, one of his relatives was decapitated, he knew the travails of hard physical labour, he was betrayed by his closest friends, he knew the loneliness of singleness, he wept as friends died, he was tortured, he had to see the pain on his mother's face as she watched him die. Nothing in his appearance drew us to him, he was hated, he was scorned, jeered, he was so unpopular crowds chanted for him to be killed... Maybe some of us have suffered more than him, but not many. How many of us can honestly say we have suffered sorrow almost to the point of death? How many can say our sorrow was so great we sweated drops like blood? Jesus, then, understands. He wants us to come to him, he wants to hold us, he wants us to turn to him bearing our vulnerability and say 'hold me close'. He wants to remove our guilt, free us from our past and love us completely. He wants to be there with us when we suffer.

So how do we deal with suffering? We are honest about our feelings, we tell God, if necessary we shout at God (just as Jesus did on the cross). But whatever we do, do it *with* God and 'Be joyful in hope, patient in affliction, faithful in prayer' (Romans 12:12).

God Wants Us to Cure the World

As well as being there with us in our own personal suffering, God passionately wants to use us to help relieve the suffering of others. Perhaps God is less worried about giving an explanation than a solution. Christ came to save and redeem the world and he wants to do it through us. We are his solution. He wants us to be his hands, his heart, his eyes and his mouth to help cure the ills of the world

Why is there suffering? Perhaps we need to accept we will never fully understand! But we need to know that God cares about the suffering and wants to use US to do something about it.

For some reason it appears that 99 per cent of the time God appears to alleviate suffering by working through humans. Surely it would be a lot more effective to bypass us as we seem to make such a mess of everything. God is capable of miraculously feeding all the world's hungry and yet for some reason he prefers to do it through humans. Even when Jesus miraculously fed the 5,000 (one of the few miracles recorded in all the gospels) he gave the food to his disciples to distribute. Now why did he do that? Why did he not simply make the food appear in people's laps? It would have been a lot simpler and quicker. I am sure the disciples would have preferred it that way – it is a lot of work to distribute food to 5,000 people in the hot sun, it would have taken ages. The last person to receive it must have had to wait a very long time. It is also very difficult. I bet there were queue-bargers, and people who came round twice and got a second helping before some had had their first. It would not surprise me if there was the odd argument too. And yet God always seems to work through humans. I have seen the mess I and other humans have made of distributing food – we get in an awful muddle. Such questions as what size ration should we give? Are we creating dependency? Should we target the child or the whole family? Should we feed daily or weekly? Should the food be wet or dry? Should we preach before we give the food? When do we stop giving food? Where should the food come from, America or locally? At times I wish he would just bypass us and do it himself. (Only once I became a parent did it occur to me that just as I take pleasure in watching my child develop and just as I delight in her clumsy and awkward first steps; so too God, presumably, takes pleasure in our uncoordinated efforts at serving him. He delights in watching us develop through fumbling mistakes and ungainly practice.)

Whatever the reason, He expects us to do it. In Judges 6 the Israelites cry out to God to help them in their suffering. God hears the prayers and appears to Gideon who asks him why he has allowed all the suffering, why he has abandoned them. How does God reply to Gideon? 'I am sending you. I will be with you.' So he sent Gideon and through Gideon defeated the Midianites with a tiny army. It was a true miracle – all who were there gave the glory to God. God could have just blown up all the Midianites before their eyes, but he chose not to, he chose to work through Gideon, 'the least in all his clan'.

In the same way, God hears our cries for those who suffer and asks us to do something about it. He wants us to be his hands feeding the hungry, alleviating suffering, housing the homeless, clothing the naked, visiting prisoners.[12] He wants us to be his heart weeping for the dead, his voice advocating against injustices. And he calls us to this end.

Why, then, is there so much suffering in the world? Because, in part, we have not done enough to prevent it. We have failed to answer his call. God has tried to send us out and we have said no.

At times I swing between thinking how much good we have done and despairing at how much work remains. Plenty done, plenty still to do. Celebrate the achievements, pray for more. God wants us to redeem all aspects of life. However, looking at it simply one could divide the work into three areas:

1 Preaching the good news that Jesus Christ can save us from our sins.
2 Serving the poor.
3 Fighting injustice.

1 Preaching the Good News that Jesus Christ can Save Us from Our Sins

On the one hand, the word of God and churches have been established in the most remote areas and corners of the globe. Maper in Sudan is 120 kilometres from the nearest clinic, the nearest school, and thousands of miles from the nearest bit of tarmac. There was, however, a church there! On the first Sunday I was there I went to the church and they asked me for Bibles. Even more amazingly someone had translated the New Testament into their language and we were able to answer their request.

On the other hand, in Africa alone there remain over a thousand languages left to be translated. Who will answer the call to translate? Generation X know less about the Bible than any previous generation. Why is this? Where are the workers?

2 Serving the Poor

On the one hand, the UN and many charities have developed incredible expertise at responding to disasters. Now when people are hungry there are many who are experts in delivering food to them in the quickest time possible. Tons of food can be dropped out of planes, thousands of tons of relief food are on the ocean as we speak, being delivered to feed the hungry. Equally in the UK, billions of pounds sterling are spent each year on alleviating poverty.

On the other hand, still over a billion people live on less than a dollar a day. Still the West continues to consume 90 per cent of the world's resources. Moreover, why is it that many of those best at delivering aid are groups such as Oxfam and MSF, not Christians? Why are so many still living in poverty?

3 Fighting Injustice

On the one hand, history tells many great stories of Christians fighting and triumphing over injustice: William Wilberforce and his fight against slavery; Martin Luther King and his fight against racism; Nelson Mandela and his long walk to freedom; and more recently the Jubilee 2000 campaign.

On the other, how many Christians understand the God of justice? What does God's heart for justice mean? Most Christians would be able to answer what God thinks about the poor and the unsaved quite well, but in all my life I can not recall a single sermon on injustice. It is repeatedly mentioned in the Bible both in the Old and New Testaments. There are over a million children who have been forced to work in the sex industry. Thousands of child slaves. Many unjust systems and trade barriers which serve to oppress the poor. Why is there so much injustice in the world?

Undoubtedly the history of the Christian church tells the story of how we have failed God and the present world illustrates how much work there is still left to do. (But of course we are going to fail God and we should be gracious with ourselves. Our basic theology is that we have all fallen short, our lives and the history of the church do prove that theology. So of course we will always fail God, fail to follow his call, fail to preach his word, serve the poor and fight injustice.) Equally the history of the church tells incredible stories of how we have answered his call: we have spread his word into every country in the world, have extremely sophisticated systems to alleviate poverty and history bears testament to many examples of us courageously conquering injustices.

So why did that mother in Sudan die? Was it Gods' fault? Or was it because her birth attendants did not seek medical help fast enough? Maybe it is because Christians are too attached to spending their Sunday afternoons pontificating about suffering rather than going out there, counting the cost and doing something about it. 'Ask the Lord...to send out workers.'[13]

Why are there billions of people living in poverty? Why do injustices reign, oppressing millions? We don't always know, but we are called to work, with God, to fight it.

Notes

1. Philippians 4:7.
2. Psalm 142:2.
3. Psalm 22:1.
4. R.T. Kendall, *Total Forgiveness*, Hodder & Stoughton, 2001, page 22.
5. Phillip Yancey, *Soul Survivor*, Hodder & Stoughton, 2003.
6. Luke 22:43.
7. Job 13:3.
8. Job 42:3.
9. Job 40:4,5.
10. Stuart K. Hine, *O Lord, my God (How great thou art)*, Kingsway's Thankyou Music, 1953.
11. R.T. Kendall, *Total Forgiveness*, Hodder & Stoughton, 2001
12. Matthew 25:35-6.
13. Matthew 9:38.

CHAPTER TEN

Final Words

We undoubtedly live in a crazy, topsy-turvy world. Never before has such absolute poverty and oppression been so close to such enormous wealth. Whilst our faith holds onto the absolutes, there are also, it feels, many shades of grey with questions left unanswered. Can anyone stare at war zones or the problems that surround us without their faith being challenged?

Such challenges, however, are not new. Around 600BC another man was also perplexed, as wickedness, strife and oppression were rampant in Judah while God seemingly did nothing.

'How long, O Lord, must I call for help, but you do not listen? Or cry out to you, "Violence!" but you do not save? Why do you make me look at injustice? Why do you tolerate wrong? Destruction and violence are before me,' wrote Habakkuk. He ends, seemingly with bleakness still before him, and yet with his faith strengthened.

> Though the fig tree does not bud and there are no grapes on the vines,
> though the olive crop fails and the fields produce no food,
> though there are no sheep in the pen and no cattle in the stalls,
> *yet I will rejoice in the Lord, I will be joyful in God my Saviour.*

The sovereign Lord is my strength; he makes my feet like the feet of a deer, he enables me to go on the heights[1] (emphasis mine).

Christ told us to pray 'may your kingdom come...on earth as it is in heaven.' Some experiences are nearer heaven than others. We may walk into a church and feel a 'peace', we may use the word 'miraculous' to describe the biology of conception or childbirth, or the adjective 'heavenly' to describe a great occasion or stunning view.[2] Maybe these could be described as 'kingdom' experiences where we have felt close to some indescribable feeling that reflects the presence or transcendent nature of God or heaven.

Equally, the opposite is true. In some of the darker alleys of Darfur, Sierra Leone or Burundi, one catches a glimpse of hell on earth, where all relations, be they between man and God, human and human, or people and their environment, seem to be broken down. In the place of love there is murder, instead of abundance there is hunger; power is used not to serve but to demean and devour the human spirit; loving sexual union is replaced by rape, mutilation and child-buggery; families turn against one another; rather than preserving the environment, it is destroyed; near extinct animals are shot and eaten, trees are wantonly cut down, houses burnt, water points destroyed – and so the delicate balance of habitat is lost; giving is replaced with theft of land, belongings and livelihoods; the fear of God and his commands is replaced by lawlessness and the rule of the gun. Evil reigns. It touches our spirit and leaves us marked.

The fact it repulses us so much is evidence of the inherent goodness that lies within all of us. It is in that goodness we find God and realize our hope. For mankind will always be shocked by evil and will always respond in kindness to try to overcome it.

As we stare at any frame of life we can see both powers battling away. The titanic struggle that lies within all our hearts lies also in every field of life. In every image of hell there are also glimmers of heaven. There is no darker sight than the impenetrable eyes of a battle hardened, gun-carrying, child soldier; nothing sadder than a mother wrapping her dead child, now a malnourished corpse, in a blanket and, in numb sorrow, beginning her long walk home into the hot, hazy distance; no more horrific reports than when fathers are forced to watch their children raped; and no more revolting a sound than the cackle of a machine gun.

But also we see a ray of light and hear the voice of hope in the generosity, bravery and adaptability of human spirit. Maybe 'it requires such depths of oppression to create such heights of character'[3] but there are few things more strikingly noble, than a highly educated, capable old man in an isolated, war-torn village, remaining with his people in an effort to educate them. Few more natural sights than watching a young man herd his goats and sheep, in seemingly perfect harmony with his surroundings and environment. Few more touching moments than when gifted by a stranger with a bracelet, a meal or a similar token of love. Few sights more fun than watching a bunch of kids scamper after a ball with all the eagerness, enthusiasm, and gratitude they can muster and then giggle excitedly as they are picked up and tickled. Few fellowships more powerful than the gospel of God's love being shared and believed by some of the most materially poor on the earth (if anyone has reason not to believe surely they do).

Few faiths are more inspiring than that of a guard pouring over his Bible at first light. Few prayers are more touching than those offered to you by strangers living in refuge. Few hugs more meaningful than those given in a strong but sad embrace as you say goodbye. It is in giving that we receive. Africans have given to me. A lot of the time I felt spiritually blunt and yet came out stronger in faith and in spirit. Such is the paradox in trying to follow the Lord. It is in losing one's life that one finds a trove of precious treasures.

Surely at the core of every human heart lies a kernel of love. For spiritual giants like Mother Teresa, that love illuminates brightly and inspires those around her. For most others our love shines less vividly, shrouded by layers of other experiences, stresses and emotions which veil that instinct. For the most hardened rebel soldier we may have to dig deeper and penetrate harder, but even he will love his brother, and yearns also for love. Years of abuse, corruption, hatred and boredom may have buried that love but we have to hope it has not been extinguished. 'If he has been taught to hate, he can learn to love.'[4]

Perhaps hope, like love and faith, is best seen as a decision rather than a feeling: you must decide to have faith in God, you have to choose to love your enemy (at times even your spouse). Equally we have to 'hold unswervingly to the hope we profess.'[5]

In the Old Testament,[6] Moses, herding his father-in-law's flock, saw a burning bush in which he sighted an angel of the Lord. Only after Moses had inquisitively gone and stared at the bush did the Lord start speaking to him.

In a dialogue that followed Moses asked the Lord some difficult questions and the Lord answered with the words 'I am who I am'. The fire that never goes out, the flaming bush that never burns, the God of the ages, the one of love, in us and with us in everything.

'I have indeed seen the misery of my people...I have heard them crying out...I am concerned about their suffering...and I have seen the way the Egyptians are oppressing them.'[7] God sees the sufferings of this world. And his response? 'I have come down to rescue them... So now, go. I am sending you...to bring my people the Israelites out of Egypt.'[8]

He looks for co-workers. Moses together with God freed the Israelites. Nothing has changed. He still hears, he still sees, and he still wants to work with us, in us and through us.

Notes

1. Habakkuk 3:17–19. I turned to this passage many times, especially in Sudan when we kept a deer in our compound.
2. The English language also uses other words, such as 'charming', 'enchanting' and 'spell-bound', all of which hint at an understanding of something 'other-worldly'.
3. Nelson Mandela, *A Long Walk to Freedom*, Abacus, 1995, page 542.
4. Nelson Mandela, *A Long Walk to Freedom*, Abacus, 1995, page 542.
5. Hebrews 10:23.
6. Exodus 3.
7. Exodus 3:7, 9.
8. Exodus 3:8, 10.

All the royalties from this book are going to Tearfund's Disaster Management Team, who have employed me for the entirety of the period covered in this book. If you want to support the work of Tearfund or their Disaster Management Team, you can contact them in the following ways:

website: www.tearfund.org
email: enquiry@tearfund.org
post: Enquiries, Tearfund, 100 Church Road, Teddington, Middlesex, TW11 8QE, UK
telephone: 00 44 (0)845 355 8355

The Disaster Management Team works in many disaster-affected regions across the world. At the time of writing, they are Burundi, Democratic Republic of Congo, Southern Sudan, Darfur, Liberia, Afghanistan, Indonesia and Northern Kenya.

The mandate of the Disaster Management Team is to reduce the death and suffering of vulnerable people by supporting "at risk" groups to mitigate, prepare for, respond to and recover from natural and man-made disaster.

It is committed to building a preventative culture in the world's most disaster-prone countries, through the integration of disaster risk reduction into sustainable development policies and practice.

Tearfund has operational disaster management capability to respond quickly and effectively to situations where there are no Tearfund partner organizations or the capacity of local partner organizations is limited.